Remodeling
your
Home
An Insider's Guide

Carol Davitt

HOME
BUILDER
PRESS

A Service of

NAHB

Home Builder Press®
National Association of Home Builders
1201 15th Street, NW
Washington, DC 20005-2800

Dedication

This book is dedicated to little Matt because he wasn't around for the first one.

Remodeling Your Home: An Insider's Guide

ISBN 0-86718-411-6

© 1996 by Home Builder Press®
of the National Association of Home Builders
of the United States of America

Cover by Dunn and Associates Design, Haward, Wisconsin

Printed in the United States of America.

Library of Congress
Cataloging-in Publication Data
Davitt, Carol. 1954-
    Remodeling Your Home: An Insider's Guide / Carol Davitt.
        p.   cm.
    Includes bibliographical references.
    ISBN 0-86718-411-6
    1. Dwellings—Remodeling. I. Title.
  TH4816.D335 1996
  643'.7—dc20   95-37194
                                    CIP

This publication is designed to provide accurate and authoritative information in regard to the subject matter covered. It is sold with the understanding that the publisher is not engaged in rendering legal, accounting, or other professional service. If legal advise or other expert assistance is required, the services of a competent professional person should be sought.

—From a Declaration of Principles jointly adopted by a Committee of the American Bar Association and a Committee of Publishers and Associations.

For further information, please contact—

Home Builder Press®
National Association of Home Builders
1201 15th Street, NW
Washington, DC 20005-2800

9/95 HBP/Kirby 4,000

Contents

Figures

Chapter 7. From Foundations to Finishes

Chapter 8. From Clean-Up to Completion Certificates

Part III. When the Dust Settles: Life After Remodeling

Chapter 9. Satisfaction Guaranteed: Understanding Warranties

About the Author

Carol Davitt of Wakefield, Rhode Island, has a wide range of experience in publishing. As owner of Davitt and Company, a marketing firm, Davitt specializes in the development of marketing plans for small businesses and associations.

Davitt frequently conducts seminars at remodeling trade shows and conventions. Her first book, *Marketing Your Remodeling Services: Putting the Pieces Together*, was published in 1993 by Home Builder Press. She also writes a monthly column for *Qualified Remodeler*, a national trade magazine.

After receiving a bachelor's degree in English from Central Connecticut State College in 1977, Davitt began a newspaper career that spanned nearly 10 years, working for the *New Britain Herald* (CT), the *Hartford Courant* (CT), and the *Providence Journal* (RI). Her byline also has appeared in such publications as the *Narragansett Times, Single Family Forum*, and *Rhode Island Builder Report*.

After receiving her master's degree in business management from Rensselaer Polytechnic Institute in 1985, Davitt became vice president of a real estate company in Rhode Island. She was graduated from the Graduate Builders Institute of the National Association of Home Builders in 1988.

A certified Rhode Island teacher, Davitt is studying for a master's degree in fine arts at Goddard College in Vermont.

Acknowledgments

I am grateful to all the people around the country who generously submitted their materials, suggestions, and best wishes for this book. Special thanks to my editor and friend, Doris M. Tennyson, for her wisdom, inspiration, and gentle hand.

Reviewers

The following people served as reviewers of the outline and manuscript for this publication: Phyllis Curtis, homeowner, former consumer advocate, and Director of Social Services, The Action Center, South Boston, Massachusetts; Alan Hanbury, CGR, Treasurer, House of Hanbury, Newington, Connecticut; David Jaffe, Staff Counsel, NAHB Office of Staff General Council; Elizabeth James, a Silver Spring, Maryland, homeowner who wishes the book had been available prior to her several remodeling efforts; Marion Kenneth Morford, an old-home owner, Takoma, Washington; Suzanne Meteyer, homeowner and real estate agent, Waldorf, Maryland; Chuck Moriarity, CGR, President, Moriarity & Matsen, Seattle, Washington; Judson L. Motsenbocker, CGR, Owner, Jud Construction, Muncie, Indiana; William Rayment, home remodeling consultant, Bellevue, Washington; Michael Strauss, Associate Editor, *Nation's Building News*, and William Young, Director, Consumer Affairs, both in the NAHB Public Affairs Division.

The following people also reviewed the outline: Geoffery Cassidy, Assistant Director, NAHB Remodelors® Council; Edward W. McGowan, CGR, President, McGowan Corporation, Binghamton, New York; Bryan Patchan, Executive Director, NAHB Remodelors® Council, National Association of Home Builders.

In addition these people provided help with the particular issues: Regina Soloman, Director, NAHB Labor, Safety, and Health Services; and Rhonda Daniels, NAHB Federal Regulatory Counsel.

Book Preparation

Remodeling Your Home: An Insider's Guide was produced under the general direction of Kent Colton, NAHB Executive Vice President/CEO, in association with NAHB staff members Jim Delizia, Staff Vice President, Member and Association Relations; Adrienne Ash, Assistant Staff Vice President, Publishing Services; Rosanne O'Connor, Director of Publications; Doris M. Tennyson, Director of Special Projects/Senior Editor and Project Editor; David Rhodes, Art Director; John Tuttle, Publications Editor; and Carolyn Kamara, Editorial Assistant.

An Insider's View

One day, while this book was still in the planning stage, I sat down to begin work on the outline. I had just settled into a chair with my 4-month-old son on my lap and my 2-year-old daughter at my feet, when I was interrupted by a knock on the door. Our electrician, Angelo Sauro, Jr., and his assistant, Gary Palumbo, had arrived to hard-wire seven smoke detectors in our two-story colonial. While preparing dinner the night before, a fast-boiling pan of water and butter ignited. As the house filled with smoke, my 7-year-old daughter responded, not the battery-operated smoke detectors. Needless to say, the situation demanded improvement.

Although I consider myself a veteran of home improvement because I have lived through countless remodeling projects and upheavals over the last 20 years, I was caught completely off guard by this seemingly simple task. Within minutes, Angelo and Gary had transformed just-vacuumed floors into heaps of chisels, utility knives, toolboxes and belts, electric drills, screwdrivers, snakes, ladders, mounds of coiled wire, and dust, plenty of it. Obviously I hadn't paid attention to my husband's early morning reminder to prepare for Angelo. Here I was, knee-deep in dust and debris, feeling overwhelmed and panicky because I had failed to plan ahead.

I salvaged the morning by rethinking my expectations. I was not going to clean the house, leave my toddler unattended, or talk on the phone. I was going to laugh a little louder, hang out with my kids, and know that, in the end, my home would be a safer place.

Plan Ahead

I tell you this story because it best conveys my purpose for writing this book. Even the smallest remodeling project can disrupt your routine and upset your emotional balance if you're not prepared. This book was written to give you the tools necessary to work with a professional remodeler, to understand the remodeling process, and to remain active throughout it.

The Remodeling Process

Technically a remodeling project has no clear-cut beginning, middle, or end. The process begins long before the first nail is driven and continues for some time after the crews have left. However each remodeling project is organized in a logical way. Surprises will certainly crop up. But the more you know about the process, the better prepared you will be to deal with these situations. The chapters in this book parallel the steps normally found in a remodeling project.

Chapter 1. Find out where to look for remodeling ideas. Whether you are planning to update a bath, undergo a whole-house remodeling, or something in between, this chapter reveals some of the obvious (and not so obvious) sources for design and product ideas. Learn how to create and organize a resource file.

Chapter 2. Are you unsure about how to find a professional remodeler? This chapter points you in the right direction. Learn how to make your decision based on professionalism using a 12-point checklist. Understand the educational designations carried by professional remodelers and discover the advantages of working with a design-build firm.

Chapter 3. How much can you afford? Whether you plan to borrow the funds or use cash on hand, decide in advance how much you can spend on your project. Find out why you need this information as soon as possible in the process. Discover some creative financing options and strategies for approaching lenders.

Chapter 4. Who will put your remodeling dreams on paper? This chapter walks you through the design process. Discover ways to make your designs more cost-effective.

Chapter 5. What information goes into a remodeling contract? What are your responsibilities? What are the remodeler's responsibilities? Learn what to include in the contract and why you should not rely on handshakes and oral promises.

Chapter 6. From permitting to packing and preparation, this chapter kicks off the production process. Learn which product decisions you must make first and which issues to raise at your preconstruction meeting. Find out how the activity curve may influence your mood.

Chapter 7. This chapter takes you, step by step, through the critical middle of a remodeling project. From site preparation to finish work, learn the materials that go into a home, the tasks that occur simultaneously, and what your responsibilities are.

Chapter 8. At last the end is in sight, but you're not finished yet. Find out why the final days of a remodeling project are so critical. Learn how to avoid costly mistakes.

Chapter 9. Most remodeling problems occur within the first year after completion. After the dust settles, if you need to, whom do you call to correct flaws in the work or the materials? This chapter explains the terms and conditions of various warranties.

Glossary. Do you know what an allowance is? Do you know the difference between a footing and a footprint? Do sheathing and shims give you the shivers? Remodeling has its own vocabulary, so a glossary is included to strengthen your understanding. But the glossary is not a substitute for your questions. If a word or expression is unfamiliar to you, ask your remodeler, subcontractor, or vendor to clarify its meaning.

Selected Bibliography. In addition to this book, many other books, pamphlets, and magazines can provide valuable information.

Sources. You will find professional organizations, software, a video, and other resources. The more information you have, the better equipped you'll be to make the decisions that will yield a first-rate project.

Worksheets. In a sense this is a how-to book with lessons designed to help you work effectively with a professional remodeler. You're more likely to experience a satisfying project if you view yourself as a member of the remodeling team. You'll find over two dozen checklists and forms. These worksheets are the ones I have developed and used throughout numerous remodeling projects.

Personal Messages. Throughout the book, you'll also read words of wisdom and encouragement from homeowners, remodelers, and other professionals from around the country. Their messages are filled with useful strategies, suggestions, and common sense. Each contributor has provided a vital piece of the puzzle to help demystify the remodeling process.

Food for Thought

Interest in remodeling has never been greater. By the year 2000, 53 million American houses will be over 20 years old, waiting to be remodeled. According to David M. Sauer, president and publisher of the trade magazine, *Qualified Remodeler*, "The average American home was built in the 1960's making [it] . . . 27 years old. Our aging structures inventory will drive a remodeling boom. Nearly three used homes change hands each year for every new one built."

Regionally those statistics mean that the average home in the Northeast is 42 years old, followed by the Midwest at 35, the West at 25, and the South at 24. If you are an owner of one of these aging structures (or you plan to be one), you may be dissatisfied with some aspect of the

Buyers of those 60's homes like the neighborhoods but are seldom satisfied with the kitchen, bathrooms, recreational areas, decorating, closets, and energy efficiency.

—David M. Sauer, President and Publisher, *Qualified Remodeler*

property (Figure I-1). Remodeling can turn your home into the one you have always wanted. This book will suggest ideas for specific changes.

Remodeling is often referred to as home improvement. This book will provide helpful information on how you can improve the various parts of your home.

Kitchens

No book on remodeling would be complete without a discussion of the most talked-about room in the house—your kitchen. If you are the beneficiary of a kitchen from the 60s or earlier, you might want to replace your simple plywood box cabinets with the sleek lines of European-style cabinets. Perhaps your existing floorplan no longer meets your needs. Today's remodelers are experts at developing and creating efficient kitchen layouts. Because it is often the most-lived in room in people's homes, few remodeling projects come close to matching the excitement of a kitchen transformation.

Bathrooms

Look at the pictures in magazines of most bathrooms before they are remodeled, and you're likely to find several common elements. In addition to dark, cramped quarters, you may see a medicine cabinet with integral lighting, a worn cast-iron tub, a wall-mounted sink, and maybe even a stand-up radiator. Today's spacious and more lavish baths can incorporate freestanding, open showers; semicircular showers; multiple vanities; and wood-framed mirrors.

Kitchens, baths, and room additions are the most popular projects homeowners undertake.

—Eric Benderoff, Editor,
Professional Builder

Bedrooms

Dreaming of a master bedroom suite? Few older homes provide their chief occupants with the kinds of luxurious spaces found in today's newer homes. If you long to create a special space, consider the following questions:

◆ What will you use the room for? Sleeping, reading, listening to music, bathing, rocking the baby, watching television, sitting in front of a fire?
◆ Besides bedroom furniture, what other pieces will you need to achieve the room's purpose? Couches, chairs, armoires, built-in desks, shelves?
◆ Do you have adequate storage? Would you like a walk-in closet?

Bedroom planning in your home need not be confined to the master bedroom. If you are creating a nursery, design it with your child's future needs in mind. Perhaps your kids have outgrown choo-choo trains and bunny rabbits, and you need to update the decorating in their rooms. If they are school-age, consider their—

Study Habits. Do they need desks, bookshelves, computer equipment?

Social Life. Do they have frequent overnight guests?

Storage Requirements. Clothes, books, games, and other possessions have a way of multiplying. Do they have adequate storage?

Need for Privacy. Consider dividers for privacy if siblings are sharing space. The loft in my newly remodeled family room was designed and built specifically with my kids' sleepovers in mind. At bedtime, they can climb a ladder and enjoy their friends' company without distracting other household members.

Recreation Areas

The recreation rooms of today bear little resemblance to those of yesterday. Recreation rooms, once relegated to the basement, are now more sophisticated in terms of function and design, and they serve a variety of special interests. Some homeowners are spending more time at home because they are enjoying their own music rooms, home theaters, exercise rooms, and libraries.

Decorating

You need vision when you purchase someone else's home. As a real estate broker, I once tried to sell a half-million dollar waterfront home, but dozens of prospective buyers couldn't get past the avocado-colored appliances, the harvest-gold wall-paper, and the string art on the walls. The couple that ultimately purchased the property realized the home's potential.

Vision allows you to see past room after room of dark, paneled walls and to anticipate golden hardwood floors under matted shag carpets. Don't let someone else's tastes hamper your ability to find a diamond in the rough. A fresh coat of paint and a little imagination can do wonders.

Closets and Storage

When you assess your need for storage, look beyond closets. Every room in your house (and outside as well) has the potential to deliver much-needed organization and structure. Stop for a moment and list all the things in your home that you store,

Other photos by the author

Figure I-1. Typical Neighborhoods

Though aging, homes adjacent to these neighborhood parks are close to downtown, shopping, and major highways.

Photo by D. M. Tennyson

collect, and arrange. Otherwise, you could be missing opportunities to create order out of clutter. For instance, I designed an entertainment center for my media room with space for a projection-screen television, stereo, speakers, VCR, and components. If I hadn't taken the time to figure out where I was going to store videotapes, remote controls, and compact and laser disks, I would have built a custom compartment for equipment and come up short on essential storage.

Listed alphabetically below is a partial inventory of some of the household and personal items for which you may need storage:

- appliances
- books
- camera equipment
- cleaning supplies
- clothes
- compact disc collection
- dishes
- dry goods
- electronic equipment
- fabric

- gardening supplies
- hobby supplies
- jewelry
- laundry supplies
- medicines
- outerwear (coats, jackets, boots, hats, gloves)
- paints
- photographs
- pots and pans

- shoes
- spices
- sweaters
- sporting goods
- tableware
- tapes
- tools
- towels
- toys
- videos

Energy Efficiency

Older homes are notorious for their energy inefficiency. The biggest culprits are single-glazed windows, drafty doors, inadequate heating systems, inefficient lighting, and poorly insulated walls and ceilings. Undoubtedly any remodeling project will include plans to correct these energy deficiencies.

Traffic Flow and Floorplan

Break free of the barriers created by those small, dark, separate compartments found in older homes. Discover the drama an open floorplan can bring. An open floorplan combines the functional efficiency of several rooms. It allows the entire family to pursue different activities and still enjoy each other's company.

Security Systems

According to "Stop Thieves," a March 1994 article in *Remodeling*, "More than 2 million houses are burglarized yearly resulting in losses of about $25 billion." You may want to replace that primitive window-wired security system with a more reliable one. When integrating a security system into your remodeling plans, you may be surprised to learn that protection requires more than just an alarm. A totally integrated system includes such features as lighting (including motion-detector lights), landscaping, fencing, windows, doors, locks, and alarms.

When designing your system, remember to update the other security system in your home with its smoke, carbon monoxide, and fire detectors. If you are still using battery-operated units, consider replacing them with hard-wired units.

Adaptation for the Physically Challenged

One of the most common reasons for remodeling is the need to make room for an aging parent or other family member with special needs. Before you build that addition or convert your attic, basement, or other spare room into living quarters for a loved one, ask yourself these questions:

◆ Is the person in good health or physically challenged? Physically challenged individuals may have difficulty with some or all of the following functions: walking, standing, sitting, lifting, grasping, hearing, and seeing.

◆ If he or she is ailing, who will be the primary caregiver? If you and your spouse work all day, will you need a visiting nurse or other specially trained person to help you? Will that person be hired as a live-in? If so, where will he or she sleep?

◆ Is your family member ambulatory or in need of special services and equipment? Often, special equipment such as a walker, wheelchair, or lift is necessary to maintain the person's mobility.

◆ Is the condition progressive? Keep future conditions in mind when you plan your remodeling project. For example, a walker-bound person may eventually require the use of a wheelchair. Be sure hallways and doors are wide enough to accommodate a wheelchair, and that he or she can easily reach and manipulate drawers, faucets, toilets, light switches, and other conveniences.

Your Home Office

More Americans than ever before are working at home. If you're self-employed or a telecommuter, you have special needs. If you work at your kitchen table or in a corner of your bedroom, you recognize the need for a functional, efficient workspace in your home. Before creating your home office, answer these questions:

◆ Where will you locate your home office? Can you take space from a spare bedroom, basement, or attic?

◆ What type of work will you perform there? Will clients visit your home office? If so, will you require a separate entrance? My home's main entry works fine for welcoming clients, but I would prefer a separate entrance with direct access into my office. When I remodel my garage, I plan to reroute business traffic through a pedestrian door in the garage.

◆ What equipment do you need? Phones, fax machines, copiers, computers, printers, answering machines, and other electronic devices may require electrical upgrading. What type of office furniture and cabinets will you need to function efficiently? Desks, file cabinets, bookcases, chairs, lamps, and printer stands take up precious space. Do you want to consider built-ins?

◆ Do you have to meet any special zoning requirements? Check the building codes in your town. Special regulations may govern home offices. Do you have sufficient parking?

◆ How do you work best? Are you most comfortable working in isolation, far removed from the activity of the rest of the house? Do you need to monitor the activities and whereabouts of small children? Is soundproofing necessary?

◆ Have you provided adequate ventilation? Where are the windows? Do they open? How will you heat and cool the space?

◆ How will you light the space? Does your work require a wash of general lighting, or will you need task lighting? Do you prefer natural or artificial lighting?

Vacation or Second Home

Maybe you're ready to turn your seasonal weekend retreat into a residence you can enjoy year-round. Many of the nation's older resort properties lack the amenities that many people have grown accustomed to. If you are dreaming of renovating your getaway, consider these questions:

◆ How often will you use the property? Are your heating and cooling systems up to par for the months you plan to visit?

◆ What will you use the property for? Will the existing bedrooms accommodate overnight guests? Do you spend a lot of time outdoors? Would a screened-in porch or multilevel deck suit your lifestyle?

◆ Are you considering resale? As with all remodeling, if resale is an option, make decisions that will appeal to a wide range of buyers. You may be crazy about purple laminate on your countertops, but will the next owner like it?

A Growing or Shrinking Household

If children outnumber bedrooms in your household, you may decide to expand. Or you may find yourself in an empty nest once your children have left for college or careers.

Hobbies, Storage, or Specialized Activities

Perhaps your family's interests and hobbies warrant the creation of additional spaces. When my kids outgrew their need for a playroom, I was able to combine that space with an existing sunroom to create a large multipurpose family room. Maybe you need a game room, computer center, or just a convenient place to store all your gardening tools and supplies. Perhaps you could use a workshop for making furniture, a darkroom for photo developing, or a garage for refurbishing an antique car. Begin assessing your needs now.

◆ Describe a typical day in your home. Pay special attention to the peak periods when interaction among family members is the highest. For example, describe the atmosphere in your home mornings, evenings, and weekends. You are more apt to notice stress points and areas needing improvement at these times. Do people jockey for bathroom time? Are food preparers hampered at mealtime by lack of space?

◆ List, in the order of importance, the spaces you wish you could alter or add.

Let the Dreams Begin

Whatever the reasons for remodeling your home, however large or small the conversion, remodeling requires planning, professionalism, patience, and a sense of humor. Remodeling is a personal matter and no two projects are exactly alike. However you can use these thoughts as a springboard for brainstorming your own ideas. So sharpen your pencil, set your imagination in motion, and let the dreams begin.

Chapter 1

Imagine, Brainstorm Ideas, and Plan

You've put up with that dark, outdated kitchen long enough. Maybe you've decided that you've taken your last hand-held shower in that vintage ball-and-claw bathtub. Or you could just be sick of tripping over visiting family and friends camped out in sleeping bags on your living room floor. If you're dreaming of a new kitchen, bath, room addition, or other space, this book will guide you through the exciting, sometimes confusing, process of home remodeling. (See Figure 1-1 for the best places to learn about how to plan a remodeling project.)

Where to Look

Magazines

If you're like me, home improvement magazines are the first place you turn for ideas for a remodeling project. You'll have no difficulty finding magazines that cater specifically to home improvement, remodeling, and lifestyle. In addition to *Home, House Beautiful*, and *Better Homes and Gardens®* Special Interest Publication *Remodeling Ideas,* you should also consult magazines that focus on a particular subject, interest, or activity. If you're planning a kitchen remodeling project, you might look at food and drink magazines that appeal to gourmets and health-conscious individuals. Publications such as *Cooking Light, Gourmet*, and *Food and Wine* often feature photographs of beautifully appointed and equipped kitchens. If you like a particular style (country, for example), examine magazines that address that lifestyle, such as *Country Home®, Country Living,* and *Mary Emmerling's Country.* Women's magazines, such as *Ladies' Home Journal®, Family Weekly,* and *Good Housekeeping*, also provide glimpses into all kinds of styles of American kitchens.

If you want your new spaces to blend with the rest of your home and surroundings, you need to give landscaping the careful attention it deserves. Magazines such as *Fine Gardening* and *Better Homes and Gardens®* feature regular sections on landscaping and gardening. Another option is to consult seed catalogs, bulb

Figure 1-1. Remodeling Ideas

[When planning a remodeling project, take advantage of all the resources available. Use this worksheet to explore alternatives and begin organizing your ideas.]

Magazines. Which publications should you buy, and which can you borrow from a friend or the library?

Title   **Location**

_____   _____

_____   _____

_____   _____

Books. Check the library or bookstore for appropriate titles, and collect manuals for the various materials you hope to use (see Selected Bibliography).

Title   **Author**

_____   _____

_____   _____

_____   _____

Home and Mall Shows. Call your local convention center or business organization for the date of the next home and mall shows in your area. _____

_____

Friends, Family, and Neighbors. List acquaintances who have recently had work done on their homes and call them. They may have experiences and publications to share.

_____

_____

_____

Suppliers. Visit your local building materials supplier or hardware store and gather free materials, such as paint and stain charts, wallcovering books, leaflets, and brochures.

_____

_____

_____

(Continued)

Figure 1-1. Remodeling Ideas (Continued)

Home Buyer's Fairs. Check with your local Board of Realtors for the next home buyer's fair in your area. Ask for a list of exhibitors, participants, seminars, and other activities.

_____

_____

_____

Remodeling Professionals. Most remodeling professionals have libraries of product ideas, designs, and materials. If you already are working with a remodeler, ask to borrow from his or her collection. _____

_____

_____

Architects. If you have already chosen an architect or designer, ask to borrow some of his or her literature. _____

_____

_____

Observation. List neighboring houses and/or areas you would like to visit for ideas.

Location	Town	Purpose

Newspapers. Clip relevant articles about the type of project you will undertake. Contact your local newspaper for the dates of upcoming special home improvement sections.

Name of Publication	Name of Section	Date

Figure 1-2. Sources of Ideas

Magazines offer an endless supply of home improvement ideas.

Photo by the author

distributors, and fencing companies for ideas for backyards, patios, gardens, and walkways (Figure 1-2).

To save money, you could try to borrow your favorites from a friend or the public library. Of course, you will not be able to clip any of the pictures or articles. Unless you are trying to match a color, most pages will copy quite nicely on a well-maintained copy machine. Check with your librarian first to avoid infringing on any copyrights. (For more information on organizing and storing information, see Organize Your Files later in this chapter.)

Special sections in the back of many magazines offer further help in locating information. Look for and take advantage of these special sections, discussed below.

Resources. Buying guides in magazines contain information about products and services in each issue. They usually include the names, addresses, and toll-free phone numbers of manufacturers, architects, designers, and contractors.

Information to Order. You can request a wide range of free or inexpensive literature by completing the mail-in coupons inserted in magazines.

Sketches and Floor Plans. No two remodeling projects are the same, but you can gain some insight into how another homeowner solved a space problem by carefully studying sketches and floor plans. If you are easily confused by plans and drawings (initially many people are), imagine yourself in the middle of the room or space on the plan. I find this kind of visualization helps me reduce distractions and encourages concentration.

Advertisements. The most obvious place to find information about new products and how you can use them is in the manufacturers' advertisements in these magazines.

Books

Browse in a bookstore with a well-stocked home improvement section, but beware of books that tell you to be your own remodeling contractor. Unless you're highly skilled and licensed in all the trades, you could be getting in over your head. Most remodeling projects call for a level of skill and workhours beyond those stated in these books. As you will see in Chapter 2, the job of a professional remodeler requires experience and competence in a wide range of disciplines.

Remember, too, to consult product manuals, which you can obtain from building materials suppliers and hardware and other stores or by writing to the manufacturer of the particular product.

Newspapers

Many newspapers now publish regular sections devoted to real estate, home design, and home improvement. In addition twice a year—usually in the spring and fall—most newspapers publish special home improvement supplements. All these contain timely articles and useful advertisements on home improvement, repair, and maintenance.

Friends, Family, and Neighbors

Do you know someone who has recently remodeled his or her home in a style you admire? He or she may still have product manuals, magazines, and other helpful information you can borrow, as well as practical advice drawn from his or her own experience.

Remodeling Professionals

Your remodeler or builder can offer you lots of planning assistance with his or her library of product manuals, magazines, brochures, and blueprints. This help is one of the advantages of choosing a remodeler as soon as possible (see other advantages in Chapter 2). If you're already working with a designer or architect, ask to borrow from that firm's extensive collection of printed material.

Suppliers

Lumberyards, hardware stores, and other suppliers can be valuable sources of information (but not, of course, as substitutes for a consultation with a professional remodeler). Many of these suppliers now offer home planning centers, where you can browse comfortably among plan books, product manuals, sourcebooks, mortgage information, building tips, magazines, brochures, and listings of participating local remodelers and builders. A fairly new center in West Kingston, Rhode Island, is receiving a lot of attention from consumers and remodelers alike. Consumers appreciate the convenience of having all this information in one place, and remodelers value the opportunity to meet prospective clients (Figure 1-3).

Observation

Once you've decided to remodel your home, keep a loaded camera and some extra film in your vehicle. I never know when a trip to the grocery store might net me a glimpse of just the right exterior door or window trim, so I go prepared. If you're

Courtesy of Arnold Lumber Company, West Kingston, Rhode Island

Figure 1-3. Home Planning Center

Many essential tools for planning a home remodeling project can be found inside this comfortable home planning center.

planning a restoration project, you might want to visit a particular historic district in your area and photograph some exteriors.

Home and Mall Shows

Contact your local convention center or business organization for a schedule of up-coming home shows. Home shows are a great source for preliminary research on products and materials. Be sure to bring a large tote bag or book bag because most exhibitors have materials for you to take home. Home shows allow you to gather a lot of information quickly. Depending on the size of the show and the distance I have to travel to attend, I try to visit several times. The first day I scan the whole exhibit and gather information. I spend an evening or part of the next day reviewing my materials. When I return to the show, I'm better prepared to ask questions.

Home Buyer's Fairs

Remodelers, builders, real estate agents, lenders, and appraisers often pool their resources to sponsor local home buyer's fairs. Even though you're not buying a new home, much of the information you can gather at these fairs can help you in making your remodeling decisions. You may even meet your future remodeler there. Take advantage of the short, informal seminars provided and pick up plenty of printed material.

Computer Software

Builder magazine, a trade publication for the nation's professional builders and remodelers, publishes an "Annual Buyer's Guide" in the April issue. This guide provides information about 5,200 building products and more than 1,750 manufacturers. If you have a computer with enough memory to handle CD-ROM disks, the magazine sells a CD-ROM version of the "Annual Buyer's Guide." This electronic version provides information about 26 product categories—from appliances to windows. At the touch of a button on your computer, you can gain access to manufacturers' addresses and phone numbers, product descriptions, and catalogs (see Selected Bibliography).

What to Look for

As you plan your project, move from the general to the specific while you keep an eye on the overall idea and the money you can spend. In remodeling, because one decision piggybacks another, costs can rise quickly, so having the whole picture in mind simplifies the process. For example, you may have picked out kitchen cabinets, but have you decided on the style of hardware? Did you know that round knobs are harder to hold than D-shaped handles? When possible, I test my selections in the supplier's showroom before making my final decision.

If you're remodeling your kitchen or bath or creating a home office or any other area where work surfaces will be necessary, consider your countertops. Will you use laminate, granite, solid surface, stainless steel, tile, butcher block, concrete? I thought that granite was expensive until I compared it with other surfaces. Work through your preconceived notions by making your own comparisons. Pick out the general style, but don't become too attached to it until you've weighed the alternatives and consulted your remodeler. An idea you're considering may not be practical or a product may not be available locally. The remodeler may know of a better product, better buy, and/or better service, and you can benefit from his or her experience with products. I find I can avoid feeling overwhelmed and becoming discouraged in the early stages of a remodeling project when I deal with one decision at a time and try to remain flexible.

When to Look

Remember that remodeling is a process—every step can't happen all at once. Give yourself plenty of time to prepare. You and your remodeler must schedule the various steps in your project in a way that will work best for both of you. Now you need to prepare for the steps in the remodeling process described in the following paragraphs.

Permits

Allow plenty of time for obtaining permits—bureaucratic processes seldom happen quickly (see Chapter 6).

Product Selection

Depending on the size and nature of your project, product selection can be a time-consuming task. To allow time for viewing and selecting materials and products, ask your remodeler for a schedule of the deadline dates for your crucial product decisions. The more information you can gather on a particular product ahead of time, the better prepared you will be to make the best choice.

Orders

Give yourself and your remodeler plenty of lead time when ordering products and materials. Prices of major building components, such as windows, increase by approximately 5 to 8 percent annually, typically in February. Lumber prices can vary seasonally by 60 to 80 percent. If you expect your project to evolve over several seasons, ask your remodeler about the possibility of ordering certain materials before the rate increase. A savings of $150 on a window order of $3,000 may not sound tremendous until you consider the accessories or upgrades you could buy with the money saved or even dinners out.

When ordering custom cabinets, give yourself at least 4 to 6 weeks for delivery. In some cases, we don't even begin a job for 3 to 4 weeks.

—Scott Grinnell, Grinnell Cabinetmakers, Cranston, Rhode Island

When ordering custom items such as cabinets, pay attention to the turnaround time quoted by the manufacturer. You probably won't want your old cabinets torn out immediately if delivery of the new ones will take 4 to 6 weeks.

Weather

Consider the seasons and whether your house would be exposed to extremely cold, hot, wet, or windy weather and the protection needed. Can you plan exposure to weather when the temperature is warm to conserve heat or cool to save on air conditioning? Obviously you wouldn't want to remove your roof during hurricane season.

Environmental and Health Issues

Note any environmental or health issues your remodeler may need to help you with, such as finding experts to dispose of radon, lead, asbestos, and volatile organic compounds. The Environmental Protection Agency offers an information pamphlet, *A Citizen's Guide to Radon: What It Is and What to Do About It* (see Selected Bibliography).

Hazardous Materials. Homes built before 1978 often contain hazardous lead-based paint and asbestos-containing materials (ACMs). Sawing, sanding, drilling, and grinding can disturb harmful particles during remodeling. Lead paint and ACMs should be handled only by properly trained, certified, or licensed abatement contractors. Lead exposure to children under age 6 poses a serious health threat, so be sure to keep young children away from a worksite where hazardous materials are being removed.

Underground Conditions. Is an old oil tank still buried where an addition will go, even though the oil furnace has been replaced? If the soil around the tank is stained, the tank may have been leaking for some time, and the groundwater may be polluted. Laboratory tests of the water will reveal the exact nature and the extent of the pollution. Ask your state department of environmental management or other local authority about the proper method of removal.

Underground electrical wires and gas lines also could pose a serious safety issue, so call your local utility hotline before any digging begins.

How to Look

When you find an example that resembles the project you have in mind, look beyond the obvious design element that drew you to it in the first place. For example, when I find a picture of a bathroom that appeals to me, I take into account all the features that make that design unique. I consider the lighting, flooring, wallcovering, windows, doors, trim, mirrors, plumbing fixtures, basins, cabinets, faucets, and ceiling. A lot of little features contribute to the total look (Figures 1-4 and 1-5).

Figure 1-4. Rendering of a Kitchen

This drawing of a U-shaped kitchen shows some of the elements that go into a workable design.

Source: Reprinted with permission from Crown Point Cabinetry, Claremont, New Hampshire

Figure 1-5. How to Look for Ideas

[Practice looking beyond the obvious and begin noticing all the elements that make a particular design work. Use a separate sheet for each room to record your first impressions.]

Approximate room size and comparison to your project _____

_____

Ceiling finish_____

_____

Lighting _____

_____

Paint color/stain _____

_____

Windows and skylights _____

_____

Trim and moldings_____

_____

Window treatments (curtains, shades, blinds, shutters, or bare)_____

_____

Bathtub (vintage, whirlpool tub, shower, or surround) _____

_____

Toilet(s) _____

_____

Wallcoverings (wallpaper, paint, tile, or glass block) _____

_____

Cabinets _____

_____

(Continued)

Figure 1-5. How to Look for Ideas (Continued)

Hardware _____

_____

Countertop _____

_____

Basin(s) _____

Faucets and showerheads _____

_____

Mirror(s)_____

_____

Flooring_____

_____

Accessories (towel bars, hot water dispensers, plants, telephones) _____

_____

Set Aside Workspace

A sizable remodeling project will involve a lot of decisions and paperwork, so if possible, set aside a desk or a table for this work as well as storage space for your materials. If you don't organize a specific space for this purpose, one day you may end up tearing your house apart to find a paint chip or scrap of paper with some vital information on it. That manageable mound of remodeling notes can turn into a mountain of frustration overnight. While the work is being done, I try also to leave one place in the house untouched where I can escape from the noise and debris.

> *You are undertaking a major project and you need to know where all your information is. . . . Dedicate a space, near a phone, that everyone in the house knows is off-limits.*
>
> —Andrea Salvadore, Innkeeper, Skinny Dog Farm, Lakeville, Connecticut

Organize Your Files

You need to devise a system for cataloging all your information, because months from now you may not recall why you clipped a particular picture. Office supply stores offer a variety of storage devices, such as index card files, pocket folders, three-ring binders, and pleated files. For example, I use a self-contained hanging file system that fits neatly in my car and is portable enough to take along on meetings with my remodeler, subcontractors, and suppliers. If you are an experienced home computer user, look into software developed specifically for organizing home projects and modify one to meet your needs (see Sources and Figure 1-6).

Related Projects

You need to decide on any related projects that can be undertaken at the same time as your primary remodeling project. These projects would be smaller in scope, support the overall project, and include such actions as installing a home security, stereo, or central vacuum system; adding closets, a pantry, or wine cellar; or redesigning entrances and hallways. (Use Figure 1-7 as a springboard for identifying your primary and secondary projects.)

Details

Once you identify the overall nature of your project, along with any related opportunities for expansion or refinement, begin to look at some of the specific details that will make the project uniquely yours. As you move through the process, your preferences will become more firm, but for now jot down your first impressions. Many of these decisions will require your remodeler's guidance and advice. He or she may need to choose an item for technical reasons, availability, or durability. Your

Photo by D. M. Tennyson

Figure 1-6. Filing Systems

Remodeling customer uses various filing systems in temporary workspace.

Figure 1-7. Projects to Consider

Look at the big picture early in your planning. Avoid missed opportunities by checking off all the projects you are considering.]

❏ Kitchen
❏ Bath or master bath suite
❏ Great room
❏ Home office
❏ Home security system
❏ Exercise room
❏ Entertainment and/or media center
❏ Garage
❏ Attic
❏ Closet(s)

❏ Sunroom
❏ Family room
❏ Porch
❏ Deck
❏ Landscaping
❏ Whole house addition
❏ Nursery
❏ Entrances and hallways
❏ Other_____

_____

remodeler can also point out price and quality differences and help you choose products wisely within your budget.

Roofing and Siding. Be sure the colors of the roof and the siding complement each other. Let your house and its surroundings complement each other too. Try to blend in with the style of your neighborhood by using a subtle color scheme. Let the details, not the color of your house, set you apart. Think of it this way—do you want the distinction of having the only purple house on the block? Check also to be sure you are in compliance with any deed restrictions or protective covenants that may apply to your property. These conditions could limit your use of colors and materials.

Windows, Skylights, and Doors. Openings provide much needed light, ventilation, and usefulness, but remember that each of them contributes significantly to the overall cost of any construction project.

Exterior Trim. Exterior trim is the ornamental signature of the outside of your home. It should complement the roofing and siding of the building.

Plumbing Fixtures, Basins, and Faucets. Anticipate your needs and choose accordingly. For example, I love porcelain sinks, but I was concerned that the porcelain finish would get scratched and chipped in my busy household, so when I remodeled my kitchen I chose stainless steel instead.

Heating and Air-Conditioning. Central air-conditioning works most efficiently with a forced hot-air heating system. Electric heat is inexpensive to install but the most expensive to operate.

Lighting Fixtures. Be sure the lighting fixtures you have in mind enhance the project. For example, contemporary fixtures in a predominantly traditional design can look woefully out of place.

Paint and Wallcoverings. When choosing paint and wallcoverings, remember that lighter colors help to make a room appear larger and brighter. Darker shades tend to shrink rooms and also can make them appear more cozy.

Ceilings. Putting a skylight in a cathedral ceiling is easier than in a flat one because you aren't required to encase the area below the skylight to carry the light down to the ceiling. The flip side is that cathedral ceilings are harder to heat and cool.

Fireplaces or Stoves. If you're seeking an alternative heat source, you might consider a wood stove or fireplace insert. Fireplaces, while captivating, invite heat loss and burn wood less efficiently. Brick and stone fireplaces generally cost more than zero-clearance fireplaces or fireplace inserts. A zero-clearance fireplace is insulated well enough that it can be installed directly over a wood floor system without the expense of constructing a masonry chimney.

Flooring. Tile floors tend to be cold underfoot. While hardwood feels warmer, carpet provides the best insulation. Pay special attention to the areas around entrances where your floors need durability and the ability to withstand wet feet, dirt, mud, and scratches.

Interior Doors. French-style doors can turn ordinary rooms into decorative statements. Pocket doors that hide in walls can provide much-needed space. Be sure hinged doors swing into dead walls, away from electrical outlets, switches, and the traffic flow through the room.

Interior Trim, Moldings, and Stairs. Think of these items as the signature of the interior of your project. These details separate a mediocre job from a spectacular one. A detail as simple as crown molding can add a touch of class to a room.

Cabinets, Countertops, and Hardware. When choosing a countertop, remember that some materials, such as granite, are more durable and can withstand high temperatures, while laminates will bubble under similar conditions. Anticipate your use of the surface, and your professional remodeler can help you choose wisely.

Appliances. When choosing appliances, think in terms of the work they perform. For example, you can choose side-by-side, bottom-mount, top-mount, and compact refrigerators, freezers, and ice makers. Cooking elements can be electric or gas cooktops, built-in ovens, microwave or convection ovens, drop-ins, self-cleaning, continuous cleaning, and commercial. Clean-up appliances include under-the-counter dishwashers as well as portable units, trash compactors, and disposers. Laundry can be done with standard- or extra-capacity washers and dryers or stackable machines for optimum use of space.

Accessories. Accessories can add organization and function to the overall design. When adding accessories to your project, consider such amenities as hot water dispensers, water softeners, garage door openers, roll-out pantry units, vegetable bins, tray dividers, towel bars, mirrors, and tilt-out bins.

Garage Doors. Unless you have a reason for calling attention to your garage, the door should be unobtrusive and harmonize with the rest of the structure. If home security is a concern, avoid doors with windows.

Landscaping. A landscaping plan can tie the whole remodeling project together and make the difference between an addition that sticks out and one that blends with the existing structure. Think ahead and talk to landscaping experts about what you want the finished landscape to look like. You might need to do the landscaping one way in the spring and another way in the fall. Prices may also vary considerably because landscaping work peaks seasonally.

Decks. Well-designed decks and patios can increase the outside living space of your home and add to its attractiveness. You'll want to integrate your deck or patio with existing structures and landscaping.

Central Vacuums and Air-Cleaning Systems. Minimize your housecleaning efforts by installing timesaving systems such as a central vacuum and an air-cleaning system as part of the remodeling project (Figure 1-8).

Figure 1-8. Product Decisions

[One remodeling decision often affects another. Use this form to check your preferences.]

Siding
- ❏ Match existing
- ❏ Change

Roofing
- ❏ Match existing
- ❏ Change to—
  - ❏ Wood
  - ❏ Rubber
  - ❏ Gravel
  - ❏ Tar
  - ❏ Asphalt
  - ❏ Other _____

Chimney
- ❏ Brick
- ❏ Stone
- ❏ Wood
- ❏ Stucco
- ❏ Stovepipe
- ❏ Other _____

Windows
- ❏ Double-hung
- ❏ Casement
- ❏ Removable grilles
- ❏ True divided-light
- ❏ Wood
- ❏ Vinyl- or aluminum-clad
- ❏ Awning
- ❏ Sliding

- ❏ Bow
- ❏ Arched
- ❏ Circle top
- ❏ Combination
- ❏ Stained or leaded glass
- ❏ Other _____

Skylights
- ❏ Fixed
- ❏ Fixed, venting
- ❏ Operating
- ❏ Domed
- ❏ Flat
- ❏ Pleated shades
- ❏ Extension pole
- ❏ Screens
- ❏ Other _____

Exterior Doors
- ❏ Wood
- ❏ Steel
- ❏ Molded
- ❏ Panels with or without lights
- ❏ Full view
- ❏ No glass
- ❏ Stain or paint grade
- ❏ Hardware
- ❏ Door knocker
- ❏ Kickplate
- ❏ Hinged patio

- ❏ Sliding patio
- ❏ Other _____

Exterior Trim
- ❏ Match existing
- ❏ Change

Plumbing Fixtures
- ❏ Toilet(s)
- ❏ Colors _____
  _____
- ❏ Options
  - ❏ One-piece
  - ❏ Two-piece
  - ❏ Low-flow
  - ❏ Elevated for the physically challenged
- ❏ Tubs
  - ❏ Cast iron
  - ❏ Fiberglass
  - ❏ Acrylic
  - ❏ Tub-shower unit
  - ❏ Shower
  - ❏ Hot tub
  - ❏ Whirlpool tub
  - ❏ Grab bars
  - ❏ Other _____
- ❏ Basins
  - ❏ Porcelain
  - ❏ Solid surface

(Continued)

Figure 1-8. Product Decisions (Continued)

❏ Stainless steel
❏ Drop-in
❏ Undermounted
❏ Other _____
❏ Faucets and showerheads
  ❏ Single handle
  ❏ Dual handle
  ❏ Chrome
  ❏ Brass
  ❏ Colors _____
  _____
  ❏ Pull-out spray
  ❏ Other _____

Heating and Air-Conditioning

❏ Oil
❏ Gas
❏ Electric
❏ Radiant heat
❏ Solar
❏ Heat pump
❏ Forced hot water
❏ Forced hot air
❏ Central air
❏ Window-mounted air-conditioning units (including portable units)
❏ Wall-mounted air-conditioning units
❏ Other _____

Lighting Fixtures

❏ Interior
❏ Exterior
❏ General
❏ Task
❏ Accent
❏ Recessed
❏ Track
❏ Chandelier

❏ Wall sconces
❏ Under cabinet
❏ Ceiling
❏ Wall mounted
❏ Lights on ceiling fans
❏ Pendant
❏ Portable lamps
❏ Fluorescent
❏ Halogen
❏ Other _____

Paint and Wallcoverings

❏ Match existing
❏ Change
❏ Exterior colors _____
_____
❏ Interior colors _____
_____
  ❏ Gloss
  ❏ Semigloss
  ❏ Flat
  ❏ Eggshell
  ❏ Satin
  ❏ Wallpaper _____
  _____
  ❏ Other _____

Ceilings

❏ Texture
  ❏ Smooth
  ❏ Sand
❏ Type
  ❏ Vaulted
  ❏ Cathedral
  ❏ Flat

Ceiling Fans

❏ With lights
❏ Without lights

Fireplaces or Stoves

❏ Brick

❏ Color _____
❏ Stone
  ❏ Type _____
  ❏ Mortar _____
❏ Mantel
❏ Surround

Flooring

❏ Carpets
  ❏ Style _____
  ❏ Color _____
  ❏ Stain protection ___
  _____
❏ Tile and grout
  ❏ Size _____
  ❏ Pattern _____
  ❏ Color _____
❏ Texture _____
❏ Hardwood
  ❏ Type
  ❏ Width
  ❏ Finish _____
❏ Vinyl
  ❏ Color _____
  ❏ Pattern _____
  ❏ Seamless
  ❏ Tile _____
❏ Other

Interior Doors

❏ Hollow
❏ Solid
❏ Wood
❏ Masonite
❏ Paneled
❏ Flush
❏ Bifold
❏ Pocket
❏ Louver
❏ Half-louver

(Continued)

Figure 1-8. Product Decisions (Continued)

❏ French
❏ Other _____

Interior Trim and Moldings
❏ Chair rails
❏ Doors
❏ Windows
❏ Ceilings
❏ Baseboards

Cabinets
❏ Wall and base cabinets
❏ Face-frame construction
❏ Frameless construction
❏ Stock
❏ Semicustom
❏ Custom
❏ Wood
  ❏ Ash
  ❏ Beech
  ❏ Birch
  ❏ Cherry
  ❏ Hackberry
  ❏ Hickory
  ❏ Pecan
  ❏ Maple
  ❏ Poplar
  ❏ Oak
  ❏ Walnut
  ❏ Other _____
❏ Finish
  ❏ Paint
  ❏ Stain
  ❏ Clear
  ❏ Laminate
  ❏ Other _____

Countertops
❏ Laminate
❏ Solid surface
❏ Granite

❏ Stainless steel
❏ Tile
❏ Butcher block
❏ Other _____

Hardware
❏ Functional
❏ Aesthetic
❏ Hinges
❏ Knobs
❏ Pulls
❏ Other _____

Appliances
❏ Gas
❏ Electric
❏ Built-in
❏ Colors _____
_____
_____

Accessories
❏ Hot water dispenser
❏ Trash compactor
❏ Disposal
❏ Waste chute system
❏ Appliance garage
❏ Pot and lid racks
❏ Bread drawer
❏ Roll-out unit
❏ Other _____

Mirrors
❏ Beveled
❏ Framed
❏ Unframed
❏ Shape
  ❏ Round
  ❏ Square
  ❏ Rectangular
  ❏ Geometric
  ❏ Other _____

Stairs
❏ Open
❏ Closed
❏ Iron
❏ Circular
❏ Balusters
❏ Newel posts
❏ Handrail
❏ Treads
❏ Risers and stringers
❏ Finish
  ❏ Painted
  ❏ Stained
  ❏ Carpeted
    ❏ Style _____
    ❏ Color _____
    ❏ Protection _____

Garage Doors
❏ Flush
❏ Panels
❏ Windows
❏ Opener
❏ Other _____

Landscaping
❏ Orientation _____
❏ Selection _____
❏ Site _____

Decks
❏ Purpose _____
❏ Size _____
❏ Design _____
❏ Shape _____
❏ Materials _____
❏ Location _____

Central Vacuum System
❏ Yes ❏ No

Air-Cleaning System
❏ Yes ❏ No

Remodeling Memories

Decide how you will preserve your remodeling memories. Will you take before-during-and-after photographs? Perhaps you can videotape segments of the job at key times. For instance, if you add a fireplace and a bay window with a window seat to your family room, you might make a video at a family gathering and show people sitting in front of the fireplace and on the window seat. You also might videotape your remodeler explaining various aspects of the job as you take friends on a tour during an open house celebrating the job's completion.

The originals of the photographs and/or the video help to establish a new tax base for your house and should be stored in your safe-deposit box for insurance purposes (Figure 1-9).

When you are ready to enlist the help of a professional, select the remodeler the same way you select your project—with a thorough examination of your needs and an eye toward excellence.

Figure 1-9. Before and After

Notice the dramatic improvement in this beach bungalow.

Photos by the author

Chapter 2

Ask an Expert:
Find a Professional Remodeler

If you've ever attempted your own home improvement project and been disappointed with the results and the process itself, you know the importance of choosing a professional for the job. Even if you were dazzled with the results, chances are the project required more time and money than you originally anticipated. Truth is, most remodeling projects involve a level of expertise most do-it-yourself advocates fail to recognize.

Why You Need a Professional Remodeler

Remodeling is a full-time profession, and those who practice it must be experts in many matters. The professionals' many qualities, abilities, and areas of experience include—

◆ vision (the ability to see the whole picture)
◆ construction know-how
◆ scheduling experience
◆ financial management experience
◆ knowledge of materials and their performance
◆ a network of suppliers and subcontractors
◆ access to innovative products and techniques
◆ access to a skilled labor pool
◆ tools

Once you decide to proceed with your project, select a professional remodeler as soon as possible. When you have assessed his or her qualities, you can work together to develop and build the best project possible with the best materials available.

Vision

The remodeler you select should have the ability to see the whole picture. While each remodeling project is unique, most follow a logical sequence of events. Your remodeler should be able to gauge the approximate amount of time the project will take, identify the nature of the disruptions to your daily living, and estimate the impact on existing plumbing, heating, and electrical systems and on your landscaping. Your remodeler should be able to clearly communicate those issues to you so you can prepare for the inevitable disorder a remodeling project will create in your life. He or she will know which problems can be prevented and other ways to make the job go smoother for you.

Construction and Reconstruction Know-How

Running a successful remodeling company involves more than just construction knowledge. Many of today's professional remodelers began their careers working in the field, and some of them have exchanged their toolbelts for the full-time management of their companies. If the owner of a company you are considering will not be the one actually driving the nails, don't overlook that company. A remodeler who works all day in the field must struggle to keep ahead of all the other business details that come up during the day. Estimates, invoicing, and scheduling often are put off until after hours when a remodeler has already put in a strenuous day on the site. While many fine remodelers try to do it all, managing the daily demands of production and business management is becoming increasingly more difficult.

The new breed of remodeler employs individuals who manage the field work. Be sure to meet the production manager or lead carpenter for your job before construction starts and note how he or she communicates with both you and the crew. If the person you are considering treats you with respect but speaks so sharply to employees and subcontractors that you feel uncomfortable, you might prefer working with someone else. Be sure you can communicate well with each other.

Scheduling Experience

One of the most complex tasks involved in any remodeling project is the scheduling of labor and materials. Ask former customers if a remodeler you are considering is adept at managing subcontractors and material deliveries to keep the job on schedule. Homeowners and remodelers alike wince at the thought of crew members standing around with nothing to do because they ran out of materials or because a subcontractor failed to show up. Even worse from the homeowner's viewpoint is when no one from the remodeling team shows up. Timing is crucial even on the smallest job.

Remodeling involves a hierarchy of events, a critical path of tasks that cannot be rearranged or hurried. One overbooked subcontractor can wreck your job's schedule. You want a remodeler who respects the subcontractors and alerts them well in advance of your job and schedules them accordingly. Of course, glitches should be the exception not the rule.

A professional remodeler will provide you with a schedule of your job so you can track the progress right along with management. This schedule should include deadline dates for important selections you must make, such as for cabinets, flooring, and paint or stain colors. Scheduling these decisions helps keep your project moving toward completion. A job could come to an abrupt halt if the homeowner has not made certain product or material selections on time. One way to make sure you don't hold up your own job is to mark on your calendar in one color the tasks you need to do that week and use another color for the tasks you need to do to prepare for the next week.

Beware of the remodeler who jumps from job to job to keep cash flowing. If a remodeler has to pull the members of a crew off your job and reassign them, you could experience a substantial delay in job completion. Find out if your remodeler has scheduled other jobs at the same time as yours, if you can expect a full-time crew, and how many workhours your job is expected to take.

Inform your remodeler of any special scheduling concerns you may have. For example, if you are a nightshift worker, the remodeling crew would have to work as quietly as possible during the early morning hours or perhaps start later in the day. If you work from a home office, as I do, and your income depends upon being able to use that office, you might make that space the last place to be disturbed and concentrate any work in that area into the briefest possible time. Preventing loss of income can require careful timing of both work and deliveries.

Financial Management

Trust is an essential ingredient in your relationship with your remodeler. Your remodeling dollars must pay subcontractors, crew members, and suppliers, and you must feel secure that your money is being allocated properly. You need a remodeler who is an expert at financial management, one who does not borrow from the proceeds of one job to pay for another. A skillful remodeler takes financial management of his or her company seriously and pays crew members, subcontractors, and vendors on time. He or she should know at all times how the actual costs of your project compare to the planned budget.

Knowledge of Materials and Their Performance

Hire a remodeler with enough years of experience to be able to recommend materials and products that have withstood the test of time. An experienced remodeler will know which skylights perform the best, which faucets do not drip, which dishwashers are the quietest.

Network of Suppliers and Subcontractors

Look for a remodeler who has assembled a qualified team of suppliers and subcontractors. Remodelers who do repeat business with suppliers and subcontractors receive better discounts on materials and labor, which directly affects the cost of your job.

Access to Innovative Products and Techniques

Professional remodelers look for innovative products and techniques in trade journals and at the industry's major trade shows. Occasionally a remodeler may not have an answer to one of your questions, but he or she should be able to provide the information you requested within a few days.

Access to Skilled Labor Pool

Remodelers with the best reputations have talented crews who bring their expertise and enthusiasm to the job every day. A remodeler who provides ongoing training and advancement to employees enjoys low turnover and low absenteeism and fosters dedication and commitment to the job.

Tools

Construction Tools. High-quality tools that are kept in sound condition and used correctly with the proper equipment rarely pose any safety or health hazards. Many of the tools to be used in your remodeling job—power tools, extension cords, ladders, scaffolding, staging, and others—must meet the standards of the Occupational Safety and Health Administration (OSHA). In visiting a prospective remodeler's jobsite, make your own informal inspection: Are electrical cords in sound condition (not frayed, damaged, or mended)? Do the tools look abused or physically altered (safety guards removed)? Are they carefully placed out of the workpath, left lying about, or tossed into the back of a pickup to bounce around? Are stepladders on level ground, and extension ladders securely tied at the top?

Communication Tools. A computer is an essential business management tool, and few of today's professional remodelers would be without computerized word processing, scheduling, job costing, and job tracking.

The Design-Build Firm

A design-build firm is a one-stop shop. Traditionally designing and building have been two separate stages in the construction or reconstruction process. The homeowner would first contract with a designer or architect to have plans drawn, then look for a remodeler. Today more homeowners are discovering that hiring a remodeler who specializes in the design-build process is cost effective and saves time. Bringing the two steps together can help you match your dreams with your budget more readily. With a design-build firm you also work with the same professional remodeler from the design of the project through construction.

Design-build firms can operate in one of three different ways. First, the remodeler is formally trained or self-taught as a designer; second, the remodeler employs an in-house architect or designer; or finally the remodeler has a cooperative arrangement with an independent architect outside his or her own remodeling firm.

Where to Look

Resist the temptation to open up your telephone directory and randomly pick a remodeler from the listings. While many fine remodelers advertise in the telephone book, you have many more options available for finding a professional remodeler (Figure 2-1).

Figure 2-1. Where to Find a Professional Remodeler

[Choosing a professional remodeler for your project is the most important decision you will make, so be thorough. Use this checklist to keep a record of remodeling companies, where you find them, first impressions, phone numbers, and other relevant information.]

❑ **Word-of-Mouth Sources** (Include date you gathered information, contacts made, phone numbers, and useful comments) _____

_____

❑ Family, friends, and neighbors _____

_____

❑ Lenders _____

_____

❑ Architects and designers _____

_____

❑ Building materials suppliers and hardware stores_____

_____

❑ Subcontractors _____

_____

❑ Local home builders associations_____

_____

❑ **Jobsite or Vehicular Signs.** (Where seen, first impression, phone number, and other information) _____

❑ **Local Media** (Include name and type of medium, date seen, first impression, phone numbers, and other information.

❑ Newspaper or Magazine Articles _____

_____

(Continued)

Figure 2-1. Where to Find a Professional Remodeler (Continued)

❏ Classified ads _____

_____

❏ Display ads _____

_____

❏ Radio and TV commercials _____

_____

❏ **Direct Mail** (Type of piece and date received) _____

❏ **Home and Mall Shows** (Dates attended, contacts made, first impressions) _____

_____

❏ **Seminars** (Dates attended, sponsor, contacts made) _____

_____

❏ **Local Talk Shows** (Station or channel, time of day, frequency) _____

_____

Word-of-Mouth Sources

Family, Friends, and Neighbors. Has a family member, friend, or neighbor recently remodeled his or her home? They can be sources of valuable information about the quality, progress, and result of the project. Ask about the scope of work, length of job, and the homeowner's perceptions of the remodeler, crew, and subcontractors—before, during, and after the job.

Lenders. Your local banker or savings and loan officer may be willing to provide you with the names of several remodelers with whom the institution has dealt professionally.

Architects and Designers. If you are already working with a designer or architect, he or she can recommend remodelers experienced in your type of project.

Building Materials Suppliers and Hardware Stores. Use suppliers as a reliable source for the names of reputable remodelers not as a substitute for them.

Subcontractors. Your heating contractor, electrician, landscaper, or other subcontractor may be able to offer several names of professional remodelers with whom they have worked.

Trade Associations. Call your local home builders association, Remodelors® Council, local business, or other organization for a list of names of remodelers in your area.

Local Building Officials and Inspectors. While these people are in a unique position to recommend remodelers (they inspect their work), most prefer to remain impartial and independent. If in doubt, contact your local building department.

Jobsite or Vehicular Signs

Is a neighbor having work done on his or her home? Has the remodeler set up a job-site sign on the property? A remodeler who has company signage professionally made is more likely to take pride in a high-quality job. A hastily scribbled message on a scrap of plywood could be an indicator of sloppy workmanship.

When I pass a remodeler's truck on the road, I notice its condition and cleanliness. A new truck doesn't guarantee quality, but a well-maintained vehicle is another sign of professionalism. The professional remodeler will stamp competence and efficiency on all aspects of his or her operation.

Local Media

Watch for newspaper or magazine articles and feature stories about remodelers as well as press releases, editorials, letters to the editor, and columns written by remodelers.

Classified Advertising. Check the listings in your local newspaper or shopper's newsletter, but don't rely solely on such listings to find a professional remodeler.

Display Advertising. Remodelers sometimes use new-home advertising magazines and booklets to promote their products and services because many homeowners start out looking for new homes. These homeowners may later decide to remodel their existing homes or the new homes they buy. Remodelers also often place display ads in home improvement and real estate supplements in local newspapers.

Radio and Television Advertising. Only a few remodelers use radio and television advertising because these media are expensive.

Direct Mail

Many remodelers mail invitations or letters of introduction to homeowners located within a few blocks of their projects. Ask the homeowner for permission to tour a project with the remodeler or one of his or her representatives.

Some remodelers use newsletters to keep in touch with their previous customers. If you come across an interesting one—for example, at a neighbor's house or in a doctor's waiting room—call the remodeler's office and ask to be put on the company's mailing list.

Home and Mall Shows

I have rarely found a crowded home or mall show to be a place for in-depth interviews with remodelers; instead I gather information to review later. These shows provide opportunities to see photos of remodelers' previous projects and to learn about their staff members and design-build capabilities. Some remodelers will demonstrate their computer-aided design (CAD) systems right at the show. You may even get to see your project rendered in a three-dimensional view.

If you visit a designer show house and you like what you see, find out who did the remodeling work for the show. You may also take part in a charity auction for consulting services from remodelers, lighting experts, or other professionals.

Remember that professional remodelers you meet at these shows will judge you in much the same way you judge them. Be sure your expectations are realistic and that your budget can support the project. Homeowners who have done their homework are likely to be taken more seriously than those who are just shopping. According to Dayton, Ohio, remodeler and regular home show exhibitor, Gary Porter, CR, of G. A. Porter Construction, Inc., "The people who have impressed me the most are those who have brought drawings of the room they wish to remodel or even a full set of house plans. Those who have a sense of the investment they wish to make are easier for me to take seriously."

If you are looking for a professional remodeler at a home show, first see how they treat you. Are they responsive to your needs and wants? Do they have a sample contract and a list of previous customers they can show you?

—Gary Porter, CR, G. A. Porter Construction, Inc., Dayton, Ohio

Seminars

Check your local newspaper's upcoming events section or community billboard. Sometimes several remodelers, often through their local home builders association or Remodelors® Council, will combine their resources to stage an consumer education show. A video, *How to Choose a Remodeler*, often provides the springboard for discussion and a question-and-answer period. These seminars are an ideal place to gather information about the process and to meet the professionals who manage it (see Selected Bibliography).

Local Talk Shows

In some areas remodelers are hosting the airwaves. For example, Rosie Romero of Legacy Custom Builders, in Scottsdale, Arizona, is the well-known host of a home improvement show on Arizona's largest talk-radio station. His audience can count on a patient, responsive host who provides clear answers to their questions.

What to Look For

If you are interviewing more than one remodeler, make your decision based on professionalism, not price. Remodeling is a profession, and the individuals who practice it take all aspects of managing their businesses seriously.

Figure 2-2 provides criteria to help you assess remodelers' qualifications. One or two of these qualifications taken out of context may not give you an accurate

Figure 2-2. A Remodeler's Qualifications

[Ask the questions that will help you select a professional remodeler. Use this worksheet to record a remodeler's qualifications.]

Name _____

Years in business _____

Licensed, certified, bonded, or registered _____

Proof of insurance _____

Permanent business location _____

References, letters of recommendation, and results of follow-up calls (Copy this form for additional references.)

Party contacted _____

Job location _____

Nature of work _____

Comments from homeowner _____

Written contract ❏ Yes ❏ No

Work in Progress and Completed

Job Location	**Nature of Work/Phase**	**Quality, Cleanliness**
_____	_____	_____
_____	_____	_____
_____	_____	_____

Educational Designations (Check all that apply.)

❏ Certified Graduate Remodelor® (CGR) ❏ Certified Bath Designer (CBD)
❏ Certified Remodeler (CR) ❏ Graduate Master Builder (GMB)
❏ Certified Kitchen Designer (CKD) ❏ Other _____

Professional Affiliations (Check all that apply.)

❏ Remodelors® Council of the National As- ❏ Local business and/or civic organizations
sociation of Home Builders (NAHB-RC) _____
❏ National Association of the Remodeling _____
Industry (NARI) ❏ Other _____
❏ National Kitchen and Bath Association _____
(NKBA)

(Continued)

Figure 2-2. A Remodeler's Qualifications (Continued)

Reputation among suppliers, subcontractors, and lenders (results of conversations)

_____

_____

Readily Accessible by Phone (telephone log) _____

Date of Your Call	Time	Message	Date Call Returned
_____	_____	_____	_____
_____	_____	_____	_____
_____	_____	_____	_____

Rapport (eye contact, personality, respect for all parties involved)

_____

reading, but all together, they should give you a fairly reliable indicator of whether the remodeler you are considering is appropriate for you and your project.

Years in Business

Establishing a financially sound business usually takes 3 to 5 years. That fact doesn't mean you should overlook a remodeler who looks young—his or her business experience and professional qualifications may be impeccable. Find a remodeler whose project management experience matches the scope of work you are planning. For example, if your job will involve coordination of many trades, look for a remodeler who has a strong network of subcontractor affiliates.

Licensed, Certified, Bonded, or Registered

State laws differ. Be sure you know the requirements of your jurisdiction. Contact your state's department of business regulations or licensing for more information. In states with no license or registration requirements, check with the department of consumer protection.

Proof of Insurance

You want to hire only a remodeler who carries workers' compensation as required by law and general liability insurance. This coverage protects you if a worker is injured on your job. Ask the remodeler for a current certificate of insurance. You can always contact the insurance company yourself, and the company will send you a copy of the document.

Permanent Business Location

A permanent business location is a good indicator of stability, but plenty of fine remodelers operate out of offices in their homes. Avoid a contractor who uses only a post office box and is reluctant to give you an actual address.

References and Recommendations

When obtaining references from your remodeler's former customers, be sure the scope of the work involved closely matches the work you have in mind. A roofing contractor may not be the best choice for a bathroom remodeling job and vice versa. Ask the individuals providing references if they would hire the same remodeler again. Were problems resolved promptly and satisfactorily? Did the project come in on time and within budget? If not, did the homeowner's change orders cause the overrun, or did the remodeler make estimating errors? Your reference check should also include conversations with the remodeler's lender; the local home builders association or Remodelors® Council, other organizations he or she belongs to, and major suppliers (see Sources).

A Written Contract

Even a small job requires a legally binding document that spells out the terms and conditions of your agreement. A professional remodeler will insist on a detailed, explicit document with all aspects of the project in writing. A fair contract addresses the concerns and interests of both parties. (See Chapter 5 for a discussion of remodeling contracts and their accompanying documents.)

Work in Progress and Completed

Ask to see the remodeler's work, both in progress and completed. For safety reasons the remodeler may limit visitation to jobsites to certain hours of the day such as before work begins or at the end of the day. Be mindful of homeowners' schedules and respect their privacy.

In addition to the quality of workmanship and materials, you can learn a lot about a remodeler's quality control by visiting an ongoing project. Are rubbish and debris stored in appropriate containers or scattered all over the house and yard? Dust and debris are inherent in any remodeling project, but a responsible remodeler takes steps to keep them to a minimum. For example, does the remodeler respect the homeowner's personal property by hanging or draping dropcloths or plastic dust-confinement materials over their possessions? If the space you are remodeling must be functional at the end of every workday, be sure your remodeler understands your clean-up requirements.

How are building materials treated before installation? Are windows, doors, and trim stacked neatly out of the weather, or are they left unprotected in the path of workers and vehicles? Is parking restricted to designated areas, or are construction vehicles parked all over the lawn? Do you see or hear any evidence of smoking, foul language, or substance abuse?

Professional Affiliations

Look for a remodeler who is active in professional and trade organizations. These organizations each have adopted a strict code of ethics: the National Association of Home Builders Remodelors Council (NAHB-RC), the National Association of the Remodeling Industry (NARI), and the National Kitchen and Bath Association (NKBA). Local organizations such as business and civic organizations also promote professionalism among their members. You should be able to verify memberships by phone.

When choosing a remodeler, look for one active in professional organizations. Participation means the remodeler cares enough about the industry to be the best he or she possibly can be.

—James P. Quinly, CGR, President, Country Club Remodelers, Kansas City, Missouri

Educational Designations

Most educational programs for remodelers emphasize business management as the foundation for success. Evidence of completed coursework indicates the remodeler has met the industry's highest standards (Figure 2-3).

Some of these educational distinctions include NAHB's Certified Graduate Remodelor (CGR) and Graduate Master Builder (GMB); NARI's Certified Remodeler (CR); and NKBA's Certified Kitchen Designer (CKD) and Certified Bath Designer (CBD).

Reputation Among Industry Peers

Goodwill among suppliers, subcontractors, lenders, and other industry peers usually indicates fairness, reliability, and professionalism. You will hear about it in enthusiastic, glowing terms.

Readily Accessible by Phone

Does the remodeler return your telephone calls promptly? Does he or she keep appointments with you? Is the office phone answered by the remodeler or a staffperson, an answering machine, voice mail, or a service during regular business hours? Does the remodeler use other communication devices, such as pagers or cellular phones? Most remodelers prefer that you call the office during regular business hours, but in an emergency you should have an after-hours phone number to reach the remodeler or a qualified representative.

Rapport

You and your family will be in close contact with the remodeler and the crew until the project is completed. Are you comfortable with these people? Do you communicate easily? Does the remodeler relate well to all the project's decision makers and show respect and genuine concern for family members?

If a remodeler has the necessary qualifications and a great personality, he or she is probably a fine choice. But be sure your comfort is based on professional criteria and not just charisma.

Figure 2-3. Remodelers' Educational Designations

Professional remodelers often carry the following educational designations after their names:

Source: Reprinted with permission from the Remodelors® Council of the National Association of Home Builders, NAHB Home Builders Institute, and the National Association of the Remodeling Industry.

Once you have selected a professional remodeler, build your relationship on mutual respect and honesty. Communicate your needs and desires clearly in writing. Bring up concerns promptly. If you don't understand some aspect of the project, ask for clarification. Your remodeler should be able to explain the project patiently in terms you understand. A sensitive remodeler will anticipate your needs and calm your anxieties.

If a misunderstanding should arise, move quickly to resolve it. Some remodelers have been dismayed to learn upon job completion that the homeowner was unhappy about some facet of the project. Speak up and give your remodeler the opportunity to right any wrong.

Remodeling your home can be one of the most exciting times of your life. To ensure a memorable experience, take the time to choose a remodeler who understands your needs, speaks your language, and respects your lifestyle.

Chapter 3

What's the Cost? Budget for and Finance the Project

Once you select a professional remodeler, your remodeling plans will shift into high gear. To keep the process moving forward, use this time to set up a budget and decide how to finance the project. Even if you have personal savings to pay for your project, look at some of the financing options available. You may discover that retaining your cash and borrowing some or all of the funds makes financial sense.

How Much Can You Afford?

One of the first questions your remodeler will ask is, how much money can you afford to spend on your project? This information will help your remodeler determine if your expectations are realistic. For example, if the whole-house addition of your dreams is going to cost over $100,000, and you only have $40,000 available, you must seek alternate financing or scale back your plans. You need that information before you and your remodeler spend a lot of time and money designing a project you cannot afford to build.

If you're planning to borrow from a bank, savings institution, credit union, mortgage banker, or finance company, first determine how much money you can obtain. Qualifying for a loan ahead of time saves time and disappointment for everyone.

Most lenders follow the 28-36 rule to determine how much you can borrow. Loan officers prefer to see your monthly housing costs—including principal, interest, taxes, and insurance—below 28 percent of your gross monthly income. Total monthly payments for housing and all other consumer debts (such as credit card payments, car loans, student loans, or alimony) should not exceed 36 percent of your gross monthly income.

Suppose you and your spouse earn a total of $5,000 a month. Using the 28-36 rule, housing costs should not exceed 28 percent ($1,400), and your total monthly payments for housing and all other debts should not exceed 36 percent ($1,800). This formula is only a guideline: lenders may be willing to bend the rules slightly if you have an excellent credit rating and if the forecast for your long-term employment looks promising.

How Much Is It Going to Cost?

Once you have your budget, work with your remodeler to design with it in mind. One of the advantages of working with a professional remodeler is that he or she is a skilled estimator. Your remodeler will prepare specifications that spell out exactly which products will be used in your remodeling project. Prices of materials can vary significantly, even within one manufacturer's product line. Sometimes I've been hard-pressed to notice the differences between a $50 faucet and a $500 faucet, but my remodeler is able to explain them to me (Figure 3-1).

> *The first thing you should do if you are thinking about remodeling your home is make sure you can afford it. Look at your income and expenses and figure out just how much additional debt you can really take on.*
>
> —Nancy Nauser, Executive Director, Consumer Credit Counseling Service, Kansas City, Missouri

How to Finance Your Remodeling Project

Finding the financing for your home improvement project can be as challenging as building the project itself because today you have more options. The Tax Reform Act of 1986 declared that after 1991 interest paid on consumer debt would no longer be deductible except for housing debt. This exception includes home equity loans and home equity lines of credit. Currently you can use your primary residence as collateral to finance your remodeling project and receive the added tax benefit, but check with your accounting professional for the latest regulations.

Personal Savings

According to the Federal National Mortgage Association (Fannie Mae), about half of all homeowners use personal savings to finance their remodeling plans. If you are a homeowner just beginning to think about a project, start saving now. Even small regular savings can build up money for a downpayment. If you save the $5 or more you spend for lunch every day, in a month you will have more than $100. If you walk rather than take the bus or the subway, you could save another $10 or more a week.

Equity-Based Financing

If you purchased your home several years ago and you have some useable equity, consider these three financing options.

Home Equity Lines of Credit

A home equity line of credit is an increasingly popular form of revolving credit in which your home serves as collateral. Rather like a credit card, it lets you use special checks to borrow intermittently up to a preset limit.

Figure 3-1. Faucets in Various Price Ranges

The functional differences in these faucets may not be apparent to you, but your remodeler can explain their differences.

Photos copyright Kohler Co., Kohler, Wisconsin

Lines of credit have several characteristics that set them apart from more traditional loans. The amount of credit can be reused. Your monthly payment is based on a percentage of your average outstanding balance. As you repay principal, you can borrow it again. Most lines have variable interest rates with fixed terms of repayment between 5 to 15 years. In many cases you can pay interest only each month to keep the line open.

Some plans set minimum payments that cover a portion of the principal plus accrued interest, but unlike traditional equity loans, the amount may not be enough to repay the debt by the end of the term. When the plan ends, you may have to pay the entire balance owed all at once. You may be able to refinance this last balloon payment or borrow from another lender. But if you are unable to repay the money, you could lose your house.

Home Equity Loans (Second Mortgages)

If an open-ended home equity line of credit troubles you, consider a more traditional, fixed-rate, fixed-term home equity loan. Like the line of credit, it is secured by your house. The one major difference is the predictability with which you repay it. With a home equity loan, repayment of interest and principal is made in equal monthly installments over a specific period. As with the line of credit, you can spread your remodeling costs over time, usually between 5 to 10 years.

Cash-Out Refinancing Your Mortgage

If mortgage rates have dropped significantly since you originally purchased your house, refinancing your mortgage may make sense. Instead of taking out a second mortgage on your house, you can take out a new loan, use it to pay off the existing mortgage, and remodel your house with the surplus funds. You can finance your project up to 30 years, so if you are planning to remain in the house for several years, this option may be an alternative. However the appraised value of your home must support the additional funds you are seeking.

Depending on your current loan balance and how much rates have dropped, your monthly payments on the new loan, even after the remodeling work is paid for, could possibly remain the same.

Suppose that 10 years ago you took out a 12 percent, $120,000 loan for 30 years. During the last 10 years, you paid the principal down $8,400 ($1,234.80 a month). Using Figure 3-2, let's say you decide to refinance $150,000 at 9 percent over 30 years ($1,207.50 a month). If you pay off the $111,600 remaining on the original loan, you will have $38,400 left over for the remodeling work. As you can see from this example, your monthly payment has actually decreased by $27.30.

As attractive as this option may look on paper, remember to factor in loan closing costs and the additional interest you must pay over the life of the new loan.

Figure 3-2. The Cost of Money

[To compute your monthly interest and principal payment, find the interest rate in the first column and run your finger across to the corresponding number under the term of the loan. Next, multiply that number by the amount you intend to borrow. For example, if you intend to borrow $10,000 for 15 years at a rate of 9 percent, your payment will be $101.50 per month or 10.15 X 10.]

Interest Rate	Term (in years)					
	5	10	15	20	25	30
5%	18.87	10.61	7.91	6.60	5.85	5.37
6	19.33	11.10	8.44	7.16	6.44	6.00
7	19.80	11.61	8.99	7.75	7.07	6.65
8	20.28	12.13	9.56	8.36	7.72	7.34
9	20.76	12.67	10.15	9.00	8.40	8.05
10	21.25	13.22	10.75	9.66	9.09	8.78
11	21.75	13.78	11.37	10.33	9.81	9.53
12	22.25	14.35	12.01	11.02	10.54	10.29
13	22.76	14.94	12.66	11.72	11.28	11.07
14	23.27	15.53	13.32	12.44	12.04	11.85
15	23.79	16.13	14.00	13.17	12.81	12.64

Government-Backed Financing Options

What if you have little or no equity in your home or you want to purchase a home in need of substantial remodeling? Several government-backed programs can help you do just that.

FHA Title I Home Improvement Loan

The Federal Housing Administration (FHA) Title I Home Improvement Loan, offers an excellent source of funds for improving or enlarging your home without requiring a large downpayment or home equity. You can borrow up to $25,000 on a single-family dwelling within 90 days of acquiring a property. (The maximum loan amount is $60,000 on a multifamily dwelling.)

You can use these loans only to improve the basic livability or utility of a property—including structural additions and alterations; siding; roofing; insulation; plumbing, heating, and cooling systems; solar energy systems; and interior finishing. You cannot use the funds to install a luxury item such as a pool or spa. Call or write the Department of Housing and Urban Development (HUD) for more information (see Sources).

The FHA 203(k) Program

This program allows you to refinance or purchase a home and finance the improvements with a single loan package. Borrowing limits for qualified borrowers are established by the FHA. For more information, contact your lender or FHA (see Selected Bibliography and Sources).

The Fannie Mae HomeStyle Initiative

Fannie Mae's new HomeStyle loan is used to acquire and rehabilitate properties. Available to homeowners and remodelers, the program is partially based on an appraisal of the expected value of the property after renovation, a substantial advantage. Many lenders consider only current value (see Sources).

Other Financing Options

In addition to home equity products and government-backed programs, you may be able to secure funds for your remodeling project in one or more of these ways:

◆ Borrow against assets such as the cash value of life insurance; savings, pension, and profit-sharing programs offered by your employer; or your stock and bond accounts at your brokerage.

◆ More remodelers are offering financing as part of their total service. Find out if your remodeler is a dealer for any financial institution and whether that program meets your needs.

◆ Look into state-sponsored, low-interest programs for qualified homeowners.

◆ Ask a family member to lend you or give you the money in exchange for a shared-equity arrangement. In such an arrangement the investor receives partial ownership of your home and splits the profit or loss when the house is sold. (Be sure to discuss this offer with your attorney.)

◆ Look into reverse mortgages for homeowners if you meet the age qualification. (Check with a potential lender.)

◆ If you have a sufficient credit or cash advance line on your credit card, you can consider using it to finance your project. Remember, though, that most credit cards charge high interest rates.

What Lenders Look For

Regardless of the type of financing you apply for, lenders must have confidence in your ability to repay the loan. They will assess your creditworthiness by examining three primary areas—your income, debt and other financial obligations, and your credit history. Ask your lender for two loan applications, one to use as a worksheet and one for a final copy.

While lending requirements may vary from one institution to another, you will be asked to provide some or all of the information described below. Lenders must be able to reconstruct the information you provide them. If you have not lived in your current home for at least 2 years, plan to list your previous addresses. The process will be smoother if you account for any gaps in your employment, residency, or credit history.

Employment and Income Verification

Plan to provide information about your employment, including tax returns or W-2 forms for recent years and your most recent pay stub (not more than 30 days old). If you are self-employed, you will need to show a year-to-date, profit-and-loss statement; a balance sheet signed by an accountant; and signed business and personal tax returns from the past 2 years. (Be sure to include all schedules.) If you have worked at your current job fewer than 2 years, provide the name and address of your previous employer.

Recent Bank Statements

Monthly bank statements show the flow of funds through your checking and savings accounts. Lenders usually require a list of your bank account numbers, bank addresses, and approximate balances for each of your checking and savings accounts.

Investments

You must provide a description of any stocks, bonds, and mutual funds you own, along with the number of shares or face value, the name in which they are registered, and their market value.

Automobiles

List the year, make, and model of all the vehicles you own. For the approximate value of these, consult the *National Automobile Dealers Association Official Used Car Guide*. It is available at most public libraries.

Debts and Fixed Expenses

Supply a detailed list of your creditors, including credit card accounts, car loans, student loans, child-support payments and alimony, all with addresses, account numbers, and approximate balances. If necessary before you apply for a loan, pay down your credit card balances to reduce your payments to below 36 percent of your gross monthly income.

Identification

In addition to your Social Security number, you may be asked to show such documents as a Social Security card, driver's license (if the Social Security number is the license number), last year's W-2 or 1099 form, last year's tax return, or a copy of a computer check stub with your name, Social Security number, and employer's name.

Real Estate Owned and Mortgages Payable

Lenders require information about any real estate you own, including the balance owed, mortgage holder, loan number, current market value, and your monthly payment. This information is especially important if the property being improved is also the property presently mortgaged. You must also show proof of homeowner's insurance, including the insurance company and your agent's name.

Reports from Credit Bureaus

Credit information is managed by a vast network of computers that monitors the daily flow of credit transactions. Expect your lender to order a copy of your credit report from one of the three credit-reporting agencies to verify your personal credit history, income, and employment figures.

According to Nancy Nauser, a former banker and executive director for Consumer Credit Counseling Service in Kansas City, Missouri, homeowners planning to finance their remodeling projects should obtain a copy of their credit reports from the three major reporting agencies before applying for a loan. "Mistakes can and do happen, so even if you believe your credit rating is excellent, . . . take a look every year, to make sure the reports are accurate and up-to-date."

Lenders don't like surprises, so obtaining copies of your credit reports in advance will allow you time to prepare an explanation or seek a correction if necessary. (See Sources for the names and addresses of the nation's three major credit bureaus.)

When attempting to correct a faulty entry on your credit report, Nauser recommends, "Contact all three bureaus because correcting a mistake on one report does not necessarily correct it across the board. If you determine that the information from one of your creditors is incorrect, contact the original creditor directly. When pursuing a correction, be sure all your communications are in writing."

While Nauser acknowledges that the process can be intimidating at times, she contends, "The bureaus have become more consumer-friendly, and their people can help you through the maze." Your credit health is on the line, and you have a right to the best information available. Because your credit report is confidential, you must request your credit information in writing not by telephone. If you've been denied credit in the last 60 days, you're entitled to a free copy of your report. Otherwise you will pay a small processing fee.

If applicable, supply documents relating to any judgments against you, such as bankruptcies or other lawsuits brought by creditors. You must provide a concise explanation of the events and conditions that led to any credit problems you may have had. Attempting to minimize or hide any facts will only make lenders suspicious.

Some lenders may approve the funds for a project if they receive a satisfactory explanation for the losses sustained, along with evidence from the last several years that the borrower is rebuilding his or her credit rating.

Consult Your Tax Planner

Have you considered any increases in property taxes, insurance, house maintenance, and utility costs that will occur as a result of your remodeling project? Will the interest on your home improvement loan be tax deductible? The best person to help you determine the tax consequences of your remodeling project is your accountant, tax planner, or financial advisor. Ask for tax recommendations early in the planning process so you can determine the wisest course of action.

Resale Value of Improvements

As a rule of thumb, you should avoid overimproving your home. You may really want to build a turreted room with a spiral staircase, but would it be a wise investment? Which remodeling projects net the greatest return? Consult a real estate agent, appraiser, and/or architect about which improvements will increase your home's resale value, which could help most to sell the house later, and which are typical of the neighborhood. Regional demand for particular improvements may vary. For example, in some parts of the country, gleaming hardwood floors may be in vogue; elsewhere Mexican floor tiles may be popular.

Even if resale is not on your mind today, the wise approach to remodeling is to make your improvements within the context of your existing neighborhood. We have all seen a home that—because of some off-beat design, color scheme, or detail—calls attention to itself in a less than flattering way.

According to Kathleen Phelps, a Realtor® for Pardoe Real Estate, Inc.,

When I sell a property, the one thing I am particularly concerned with is resale. Washington, D.C., is a very transient, international community, so it's not unusual for properties to turn over every 3 to 5 years. In a real estate climate like that, I counsel buyers who are planning on remodeling their homes not to overcustomize their improvements. You may be wild about a one-bedroom, palatial suite, but the next buyer may not. Keep your improvements simple and in good taste.

—Kathleen Phelps, Realtor®, Pardoe Real Estate, Inc., Washington, D.C.

in Washington, D.C., homeowners need to be "mindful of the fact that the more customized a particular improvement is, the fewer potential buyers it may appeal to. If
you are thinking of resale, keep your improvements universal. Avoid colors or
touches that are too owner-specific. There's not much you can do wrong if you are
updating a kitchen, but resist making changes to the floorplan and room layout. The
formal dining room you eliminate to make room for a country kitchen could hurt
you at resale time."

The "Cost Vs. Value" Report

One source for such comparisons is *Remodeling* magazine's annual "Cost Vs. Value
Report" (see Selected Bibliography). Each November this trade magazine for professional remodelers publishes national data on the cost and resale value of a dozen
popular remodeling projects.

The study provides the average cost of the jobs and resale value for 60 cities
in 4 regions of the United States. It also includes hints and design tips from remodelers and real estate professionals. For example, a $19,780 kitchen remodeling project
in Los Angeles, California, would have a resale value of $18,333 if that home were
sold within a year of completion, a 93 percent return. However the figures in the
report are averages and should be used as ballpark estimates rather than absolutes
(see Selected Bibliography).

Use the planning and financing of your remodeling project as an opportunity to
assess your housing needs and preferences, short- and long-term monetary needs,
and financial goals. Make your decisions within the context of your lifestyle, personal borrowing strategy, financial well-being, and tax and estate planning.

Finally, like the properties they finance, all loans are unique. Compare rates,
terms, conditions, points, settlement or closing costs, loan origination fees, and
charges for appraisals and inspections. Choose a financing package that reflects
your current financial picture, budget, and resources as well as your anticipated
financial outlook.

Chapter 4

Avoid Sticker Shock: Design with the Budget in Mind

You have an idea of what you want your project to look like and how much money you can afford to spend on it. You now need to find out how much of your original vision you can actually achieve. The design stage of your project can be the most exhilarating, but it also requires a great deal of soul-searching, imagination, and at times, compromise.

Who Designs Your Project?

When selecting a professional to design your project, you must prioritize your needs. Is innovative design high on your list? If so, you may want to hire a design-build firm that employs or has a cooperative arrangement with an architect. You could also hire a licensed architect. Perhaps you are remodeling your kitchen or bath within their existing dimensions, and you need the design expertise of a kitchen and bath designer.

Many people can sketch a pretty picture, but if the project in the picture cannot be built, the idea is not well designed. You have several options when selecting a design professional. Each choice depends on the scope of the project, your goals, and your needs.

Your Remodeler

More remodelers are offering design-build services, and many remodeling home-owners are taking advantage of the benefits. The biggest benefit of keeping design and construction under one company's roof is the ongoing communication that occurs among all those involved in these two critical phases. This arrangement helps the pieces of the design puzzle come together within budget right from the beginning.

Occasionally a remodeler may rebate some or all of the design fee if you later sign a construction contract with the firm. But the trend is for remodelers to charge for design time.

An Architect

For a large or customized project, you may want the design expertise of a licensed architect to create highly developed and inventive plans. Architects offer a wide range of services, usually for a fee equal to 5 to 15 percent of the project's budget or by the hour. Charges vary based on the services for which you contract. These services range from preliminary sketches to a full-service package including elaborate documentation and construction management. For example, on a $100,000 remodeling project, design fees could range from $5,000 to $15,000.

A Designer

If you're going to use a designer for your project, be sure he or she understands house construction. Not everyone skilled in drafting is a designer. Sound design practices involve a complex set of systems that must be integrated to work perfectly. In some states only licensed professionals such as architects and engineers can certify residential plans.

A Kitchen and Bath Designer

If you want to remodel a kitchen or bath, consider using a kitchen or bath designer at a retail showroom to design the space (Figure 4-1). Ask your remodeler to recommend a dealer or look for one who is a member of the National Kitchen and Bath Association (NKBA) (see Sources). Membership in NKBA indicates that a dealer has been in the business for at least 2 years and has a complete showroom. Certified Kitchen Designers (CKD) and Certified Bath Designers (CBD) have been in the

Courtesy of Nick Naples Remodeling Showcase, Glastonbury, Connecticut

Figure 4-1. Kitchen and Bath Showroom

A wide range of kitchen and bath cabinets, hardware, and other products are on display in this 1,200-square-foot showroom.

industry for a minimum of 7 years, have completed rigorous NKBA courses of study, and have received highly specialized training in kitchen and bath design.

In addition to providing design services, most dealers also sell cabinets and a few handle installation. If you decide to buy them from the dealer, any design fee charged by the dealer is usually waived or credited to the purchase price of the cabinets.

The Design Process

Site Visit

Regardless of the design professional you choose, the design process will begin with a site visit. In addition your designer will also want to know more about you, your tastes and preferences, and your objectives for the project. The better prepared you are, the smoother the process will be. Ask yourself, what am I trying to accomplish with this remodeling project?

Before this meeting your designer may ask you and other household members involved in the project to create separate wish lists. Discuss all your differences now because a large part of the designer's task is to reconcile opposing tastes.

Initial Design Meeting

Your designer may visit the site again to take precise measurements and make a drawing of existing conditions if one was not done during the first visit. This drawing is the benchmark from which the architect or designer will develop the preliminary sketches.

Design Contract

Some remodelers charge separately for estimates and for design. Others include the design fee in the project's construction costs. A design contract or preconstruction agreement should specify the services being provided, a description of the project, budgets, timetables, fee arrangement, and what percentage of the fee, if any, will be credited towards the contract price of the project (see Chapter 5).

Development of Preliminary Sketches

Your designer will use the information he or she has collected to develop preliminary or concept sketches. These sketches provide a starting point for the project. At the same time the designer will also work with you to develop the project's preliminary budget using ballpark estimates derived from linear footage rather than actual products (Figure 4-2).

Preliminary Design Review Meeting

Seeing preliminary sketches for the first time can be a wonderful experience, but that excitement can fade quickly if the preliminary budget indicates that the project is going to cost more than you expected. If so, work with your designer to fine-tune the design and find cost-saving solutions.

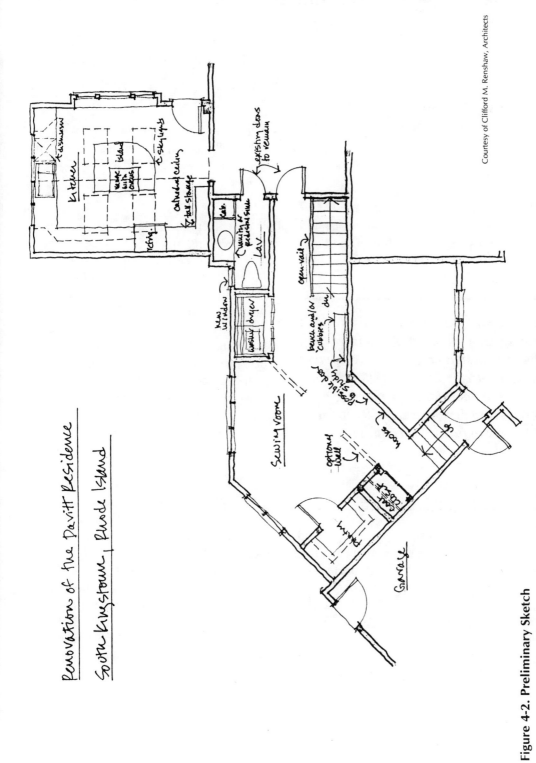

Figure 4-2. Preliminary Sketch

This sketch combines a kitchen remodeling project with the conversion of unused garage space into a sewing room, pantry, and lavatory.

Development of Working Drawings

When you have approved the preliminary sketches, the designer can develop the working drawings. The remodeler uses these drawings to construct your project. They can include some or all of the ones discussed later in this chapter under Types of Plans.

Specifications

In addition to the drawings, your remodeler or designer should provide you with a precise list of all the products and materials that will go into your project. Each item should be listed by brand name, model number, color, and size.

How to Read Blueprints

Looking at the lines, markings, and symbols on a blueprint for the first time can be confusing. I learned how to read a blueprint by picturing myself in the space, performing everyday activities and functions. Computer-generated, three-dimensional floorplans that show the design from many different vantage points also make visualization fun and easy.

An important part of residential design is furniture placement. During either the schematic design or design development phase, the architect should show furniture on the floorplan. The purpose of this exercise is to demonstrate at least one viable way to furnish the main rooms.

—Michael Knorr, AIA, and Associates, Inc., Denver, Colorado

For a more concrete perspective on blueprints, ask your remodeler or designer to take you into finished rooms of the same or approximate size as your new space. A country kitchen measuring 14 by 16 feet might sound comfortable, but if you're planning a center island, you may find the aisles tighter than you imagined.

You need to think now about how your furnishings and possessions will be arranged once the remodeling project is completed. I usually ask my remodeler or designer to draw a few pieces of furniture on the plan to give me an idea of the room's proportions.

Finally, don't let the construction terminology on blueprints confuse you. Check the glossary in this book for definitions of many of the terms used in homebuilding and remodeling. Of course, you should always ask your remodeler to clear up any confusion. Check your local library or contact the publisher, Home Builder Press, for *Understanding House Construction* (see Selected Bibliography), a soup-to-nuts primer on the homebuilding process. By the time your project is completed, you'll be speaking the language, too.

Types of Plans

Site

Your remodeling plans must satisfy all applicable building codes, zoning ordinances, and restrictive covenants in your deed. A site plan shows the location of the house in relation to septic systems, wells, underground oil tanks, utility easements, and property lines. It also provides lot dimensions and grade elevations (Figure 4-3).

A site plan may include trees and other landscaping elements but is not intended to be a landscape plan. A landscape plan (discussed later in this chapter) is another, more detailed type of plan that specifies the placement and types of plantings and decorative details.

Foundation

A foundation plan includes such items as the thickness of the concrete walls, bulkheads, footings for chimneys or lolly columns, basement windows, and any necessary drainage. A lolly column (made of cement-filled steel) supports the beams of the house.

First Floor

This plan shows the changes or additions proposed for the first floor of the house. It includes all rooms, labeled with dimensions; walls; windows; doors and their swing; stairways; cabinets; appliances; islands; bathrooms and placement of fixtures, including basins, toilet, shower, and bathtub; bookcases; and built-in storage units. Study the floorplan to determine how the project will affect the traffic patterns within the home.

Second Floor

A plan for an upper story contains the same elements found in the first-floor plan. Headroom on a second floor may be altered because of the roof line and slope.

Elevations

An elevation is a drawing of an exterior view of a house from the front, back, or sides. If the design will alter the exterior of your home, elevations give you a chance to see the project's effect from several different angles. If you are planning an addition, elevations will determine whether the new structure is compatible with the existing architectural style and materials. Elevations also show such elements as siding, windows, roof slope, chimney height, exterior doors, decks, and porches.

Cross Sections

Cross section drawings show the structural sizes of the floor systems, the rafters, and all the related materials such as insulation and ventilation.

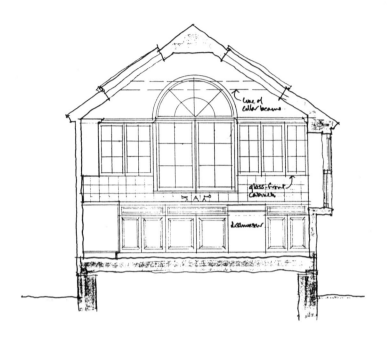

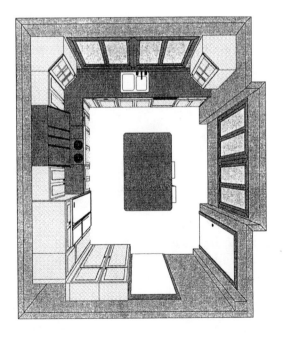

Courtesy of M and J Kitchen and Bath, East Greenwich, Rhode Island

Figure 4-3. Plans

A bird's-eye-view plan and an elevation provide three-dimensional views into the kitchen shown in Figure 4-2.

Details

Your designer will provide a drawing of any construction detail that requires a closer look. For example, you could have a detail of the interior trim around windows, doors, and baseboards. These extra drawings may add to the cost of the design.

Framing

A framing plan specifies the procedure for assembling the main frame of the project. This plan shows the framing members, the openings in the floor, and the places where an architect or engineer may want structural reinforcement for load-bearing points.

Mechanical Systems

A mechanical plan shows the placement of any ductwork. It is used mostly for projects with forced hot-air or radiant-heat systems.

Electrical

An electrical plan indicates the positions and wiring of light switches, outlets, and fixtures. Homeowners with small remodeling projects often forego the expense of an electrical plan and instead review their needs on the site with the electrician or a lighting designer. However an electrical plan takes all the guesswork out of wiring your space.

Landscaping

Think of a landscape plan as a blueprint for the outside of your home. It shows all the existing details, features, and proposed improvements, including lighting, trees, shrubs, ornamental plantings, flower beds, gardens, benches, trellises, fences, swimming pools, and driveways. A detailed landscape plan is usually contracted separately through a landscape architect or designer.

Plans You Need

If you are remodeling your kitchen or bathroom within the existing walls, you may need only a kitchen or bathroom plan. To obtain a building permit for a two-story addition, you will probably need a site plan, structural plan, floorplans, and elevations. When in doubt, consult your remodeler.

Cost-Saving Ideas

If you are willing to compromise and you like the alternatives, professional remodelers and designers know where to find budget-stretching substitutions. The checklist in Figure 4-4 shows some of those possibilities. Naturally the remodeling process contains no absolutes because for every substitution you consider, you could just as easily make an upgrade in a product that would drive the cost up. For example, a

Figure 4-4. Cost-Saving Ideas

[Use these ideas as a springboard for discussion with your remodeler and design professional. Each project is unique, and some items listed here may not apply to yours, or the materials mentioned may not be available in your region. Some of the savings may seem small, but those small savings can add up to big dividends over the course of a remodeling project. Avoid using inferior materials no matter how much money you can save. You could end up spending more money later to replace or repair them.]

Foundations

❑ Can we substitute a crawlspace or piers for a full foundation under a new addition?
  ❑ Yes ❑ No Savings $_____

Roofing

❑ How much money can we save by using asphalt or other shingles instead of wood shake shingles, slate, or clay tiles? Type of roofing _____
  Savings $_____

Windows

❑ Can we use snap-in window grilles instead of windows with true divided lights?
  ❑ Yes ❑ No Savings $_____

Glass

❑ Will limiting our use of glass (windows, doors, skylights) save any money? ❑ Yes ❑ No
  Savings $_____

Exterior Doors

❑ Can we substitute a steel exterior door for wood? ❑ Yes ❑ No Savings $_____

Interior Doors

❑ Can we substitute masonite interior doors for wood? ❑ Yes ❑ No Savings $_____

Ceilings

❑ If we substitute flat ceilings for cathedral or vaulted ones, can we save money?
  ❑ Yes ❑ No Savings $_____

Plumbing

❑ Can we stack a second-floor bathroom over a first-floor bathroom? ❑ Yes ❑ No
  Savings $_____

Fireplaces

❑ If we substitute a metal fireplace for brick or stone, can we save any money?
  ❑ Yes ❑ No Savings $_____

❑ Can we realize any benefit by installing brick to mantel height instead of going all the way up the wall? ❑ Yes ❑ No Savings $_____

Flooring

❑ Can we substitute seamless vinyl for ceramic or unglazed tile? ❑ Yes ❑ No
  Savings $_____

❑ Can we substitute carpeting for hardwood floors? ❑ Yes ❑ No Savings $_____

brick fireplace is usually cheaper to install than a stone one unless you pick the most expensive brick. Every remodeling decision is relative and must be made within the context of the whole project.

Foundations. If you are planning to add a room to your home, you may not want to disturb your yard with extensive digging for a full foundation. Your yard simply may not be able to accommodate all the dirt that will come out of the hole. If you have to pay someone to haul and dump the dirt from a 16x16-foot hole, you might have to pay an additional $400 to $600 (based on six 12-cubic yard loads at $80 to $120 a load).

Roofing. Wood shake shingles, slate, and clay tiles are three times more expensive to buy and install than asphalt or other shingles. For example, planing and fitting an 8-inch wood shingle takes longer than laying a 3-foot asphalt shingle.

Windows. The amount of money you can save using windows with snap-in grilles instead of those with true divided lights depends on the type and number of windows. Typically, a six-over-six, true divided-light casement window from a leading manufacturer costs approximately $400 to $500. The comparable snap-in version costs between $275 and $325. Depending on the number of windows you need for your project, the savings could be substantial.

Glass. The cost of windows and doors accounts for about 7 to 10 percent of most remodeling budgets. Those percentages might not sound like a lot of money, but on a $20,000 remodeling project, you could be spending as much as $2,000 on glass alone. Choose your glass wisely. For example, bow and bay windows cost much more than flat panes of glass, sliding glass doors are more expensive than windows, and French doors cost more than sliding doors. Prices will also vary for double- or triple-paned glass and low-energy glass.

Exterior Doors. Depending on the type and the style of the exterior wood door you choose, a steel substitute could cost about one-half the price of wood. A steel door also provides better thermal value and requires less maintenance.

Interior Doors. Using solid masonite interior doors, instead of six-panel pine doors, can save approximately $75 to $100 per door. Hollow masonite doors cost even less. You can also buy a pine veneer door, with pine only on the door surface, for a price in between the costs of the hollow masonite and solid masonite doors.

Ceilings. Flat ceilings are easier to install, easier to paint, and use less materials than cathedral or vaulted ceilings.

Plumbing. When you are adding a second-floor bathroom, try to stack it over an existing first-floor bathroom. This technique saves on labor and materials because you only have to run your waste- and feedlines once or connect them to the existing plumbing below. Of course, the money saved on pipes and copper will seem inconsequential if you break the budget with an expensive hot tub or a hand-painted basin.

Fireplaces. Brick's flat surface makes it less expensive to work with than stone. Stone involves more labor because each piece must be cut and fit together, like the irregular pieces of a jig-saw puzzle. You can save money by installing a brick hearth and (except for the mantel) use drywall, paneling, or plaster for the rest of the wall. Of course, your savings would be lost if you then decided to build the half-wall in teak or add a raised-panel detail.

Flooring. Oak flooring costs approximately $5 to $7 per square foot ($45 to $63 per square yard), installed and finished. A durable carpet and pad costs approximately $25 or more per square yard. Vinyl flooring used to be considered inferior to ceramic and unglazed tile. Today you can spend as much on some seamless vinyl flooring as you can spend on tile. Vinyls now come in much smaller sheets (6 feet) with matched seams. Shop carefully and ask your remodeler for guidance. The subtle differences in grades of tile and vinyl can be confusing.

You're the Boss

Your home is about to undergo an amazing transformation that you'll enjoy for years to come, so enjoy this stage of your project, too. Designing a new space, with all of its options and freedoms, is a wonderful experience. I contain construction costs by keeping the design simple and by putting some money into details—a few accent tiles in a bathroom, a decorative edging on a countertop, wall sconces instead of table lamps.

Realize that you, the client, are part of the remodeling project "team" and that you play a crucial role. You make the final choice on all decisions.

—Iris Harrell, President, Harrell Remodeling, Inc., Menlo Park, California

Give the professionals you choose plenty of latitude and encourage them to suggest ideas you haven't considered. But keep your needs and lifestyle in mind because ultimately you have to live in the space. For example, my new laundry room looked great on paper at the other end of my house, but the whole idea was to save myself steps by moving the washer and dryer out of the basement. Did I really want to walk half-way across the first floor to reach them? I kept an open mind, took a tape measure and walked the space a few times to see if the dimensions worked. Part of the remodeling process is being willing to experience new ideas. But the solution did not meet my needs, so I called a time-out to think things over (Figure 4-2).

Communicate your needs clearly as you move through the remodeling process. In the long run, compromise may be your greatest—and most rewarding—agent of change.

Chapter 5

Nail Down the Agreement: Understand the Contract Documents

Before you and your remodeler start production of your project, you must put all your plans, ideas, promises, and agreements in writing. As with the design contract discussed in Chapter 4, a well-written remodeling contract is explicit, intelligible, and fair to both parties.

Both you and your remodeler are bound by everything set down in the contract, so read it carefully before you sign. Don't be shy; the time to ask questions is before signing. If you have any questions or you don't understand a section, get an answer or explanation before you put your name on the dotted line. You also should avoid signing a blank or partially blank contract. When you are satisfied with the contract and have signed it, keep an original, signed document in a safe place for your records.

What Goes into a Remodeling Contract?

Your remodeling contract should (a) contain all the information you and your remodeler have agreed to, (b) spell out both of your responsibilities, and (c) set forth the methods for resolution if any disputes arise.

Types of Remodeling Contracts

Your remodeler's contract probably has evolved over time through a process of trial and error. Some remodelers are comfortable using the generic contracts provided by their home builders association. Others take useful clauses from various documents to create a contract that meets their unique needs (with an attorney's review). Still other remodelers rely on their business attorneys to draft their contracts.

Contract lengths vary, and multiple-page documents are not always necessary. However even the smallest project requires detailed specifications and supporting documentation. Beware of the remodeler who either insists on an oral agreement or gives you a vague or incomplete contract to sign.

Some remodelers use several contracts: one for studying the project, one for designing it, and one for construction. The first one (for a feasibility study) determines whether your project is practical before you spend thousands of dollars in design fees. Your remodeler, architect, or engineer would charge you by the hour to organize paperwork for permits, check setbacks, maybe even do a preliminary budget—all indications of whether your project will work.

The second type, the design contract, is discussed in Chapter 4. The rest of this chapter concentrates specifically on the third type, the remodeling contract.

Construction Documents

The remodeling contract is just one part of the overall construction documentation required for your project. In addition, plans, elevations, sections, detail drawings, and specifications are incorporated into the contract by reference (see Chapter 4).

The Contract

A contract describes the exact nature of the commitments each party makes to the other. A standard remodeling contract will include some or all of the following provisions.

Make sure your remodeling contract contains provisions for adequate insurance, specificity of products and materials, start and finish dates, guarantees or warranties, waivers of mechanics' liens, and a clause about who is responsible for building permits.

—Sherwin I. Pogrund, Partner, Stone, Pogrund,
Korey & Spagat, Chicago, Illinois

Parties Involved. The first paragraph of your contract should include the names of the parties to the agreement and the remodeler's registration or license number.

Job Name and Location. In addition to your street address, city, and town, this paragraph often provides a legal description of the property being remodeled, including the plat and lot numbers. Your remodeler may ask you to provide proof of ownership such as a deed.

Scope of Work. Your contract should provide a complete, accurate, and detailed description of the work to be performed with plans and specifications incorporated by reference. If you plan to perform any of the work yourself (such as painting), or if you are supplying any of the materials, this section should provide the details. It may also specify items that are not included in the scope of work, such as any landscaping you may contract for separately.

Services. Your remodeler should provide general liability and workers' compensation insurance according to state law until the project is complete. You will be expected to buy and maintain property insurance on the full value of the entire project.

Starting and Estimated Completion Dates. A professional remodeler will make every effort to diligently pursue the work through completion. However the contract may provide for extending the completion date because of conditions beyond your remodeler's control including—

◆ delays in obtaining the necessary permits or zoning variances, funding of loans, and disbursement of funds

◆ adverse weather conditions

- unavailability of materials or labor
- illness
- any act or neglect by the homeowner
- additional work or changes requested by the homeowner
- failure of the homeowner to make payments when they are due
- acts of God and similar occurrences

Contract Price. If you and your remodeler have agreed to a fixed price, your contract should state the full amount of the project. While most professional remodelers will stand by their fixed prices, you should be aware that most remodeling contracts contain a clause for hidden conditions.

Generally no allowance is made for any labor or materials needed to correct defects not readily discernible at the time of the initial estimate. Defects such as insect damage, structural damage or inadequacy, faulty utilities, and the like are usually addressed by a change order (discussed in detail later in this chapter).

You may set aside a percentage of the contract price for these unforeseen circumstances, or your remodeler may include a contingency clause that could add a predetermined percentage (usually 3 to 8 percent) to the contract price. If no hidden conditions exist, your remodeler should rebate the surplus funds. However, if costs to correct any hidden conditions exceed the money set aside, you will be responsible for making up the shortfall.

If you have agreed to a cost-plus or time-and-materials contract, you would reimburse your remodeler at regular intervals for all invoices associated with your project, plus a percentage for his or her profit and overhead. With a cost-plus contract, you would pay for time and materials as the project proceeds.

Under a cost-plus contract with a guaranteed maximum price, you still pay for the time and materials used in the project, but your remodeler sets a not-to-exceed number. It guarantees that the job will not go over a certain amount.

Progress Payments. Under a fixed-price contract, generally you would make payments or draws at key intervals as the project progresses, such as when—

- you sign the contract and make the downpayment
- work begins
- walls are framed
- the roof is shingled
- drywall installation or plastering begins
- finish work begins
- a certificate of occupancy is obtained

If you sign a cost-plus or time-and-materials contract, the remodeler will invoice you weekly or every other week for labor, materials, and subcontractors.

If you are funding your project through a bank, verify that the bank's disbursement schedule matches your remodeler's. Otherwise you and your remodeler could find yourselves at odds at payment time: your remodeler will be anticipating a progress payment, and you will be legally responsible for coming up with the funds.

Retainage is a portion of the contract price that the homeowner keeps for the purpose of leverage over the remodeler. Advocates of retainage maintain that it is an effective incentive for persuading the remodeler to finish the job. Professional remodelers disagree with this premise because a professional remodeler stakes his or her reputation on each job. In most cases, maintenance of that reputation is a stronger motivator than withheld funds. However, if you want to withhold a certain percentage from each progress payment or an amount from the final check, you cannot make this decision arbitrarily. You must incorporate a retainage clause into the contract.

Possessions. Generally the homeowner is responsible for removing personal belongings from the work areas and storing them until the certificate of occupancy is granted.

Allowances. Your remodeler usually will give you a monetary allowance for any item you have not selected before contract signing. Allowances are typically given on such items as cabinets, countertops, appliances, floor coverings, lighting fixtures, and plumbing fixtures. A tremendous variation exists among product lines, so you must verify all allowances. If you exceed your allowance, you'll have to make up the difference between the allowance and the actual purchase price. To avoid disappointment and out-of-pocket expenses, I begin shopping early for the products that will go into my project. That way, if my remodeler gives me a $3,000 cabinet allowance, and I know my selection is going to be in the $5,000 to $7,500 range, I can budget accordingly.

Your allowance schedule should state whether your allowance is for materials only—and if so, whether it includes shipping, tax, and delivery—or if it also includes installation of those materials.

Subcontractors. All the subcontractors working under your contract with the remodeler are bound by the conditions set forth in your contract. For example, if your contract specifies that your remodeler will carry workers' compensation insurance, so must the subcontractors.

Termination and Default. This section of the contract describes the circumstances under which the parties may be in default, any opportunities to remedy the default, notice requirements, and the nondefaulting party's remedy, if any. The homeowner is in default if he or she fails or refuses to pay on time any amount set forth in the contract or the contract documents; the remodeler may be in default for failure or refusal to perform the work.

Conflict Resolution. This clause stipulates the procedure for arbitrating, mediating, and/or negotiating any claims or disputes arising out of the work described in the contract.

Entire Agreement. The project and the relationship between the two parties are governed entirely by the contract and the contract documents. In other words, no other agreement or understanding, oral or otherwise, exists between them outside of the contract. It can be modified only by a written agreement signed by both parties.

Working Conditions. This section addresses various rules such as daily work hours, rubbish removal, smoking in the home, parking places, use of the phone and bathroom, presence of children and pets at the worksite, and areas off-limits. For example, my two declawed Siamese cats required special precautions during remodeling work. To prevent their loss, I had to isolate them in a separate room before crew members could open exterior doors for any length of time.

Laws, Permits, Fees, and Notices. Your remodeler agrees to comply with all applicable state and municipal health and building codes, statutes, regulations, and ordinances.

Signage. Signs assist in the delivery of materials to the worksite. They also market the remodeler's services to prospects. Will you allow your remodeler and the subcontractors to erect jobsite signs on your property? If so, for what period of time?

Miscellaneous. Generally the homeowner is responsible for such activities as confirming property lines, applying for and obtaining variances, notifying utility companies of plans to dig, utility costs such as fuel for generators, the cost of explosives (if necessary for excavation), unforeseen obstacles such as buried oil tanks, and conducting archaeological digs.

Signatures. To be legally binding, your contract must be signed by all parties. Be sure to retain one original of the signed contract for your records.

Plans, Elevations, Sections, and Detail Drawings

Your contract should reference and include one complete, clean set of the plans, elevations, sections, and detail drawings you have approved.

Specifications

Be sure the specifications describe all the details, materials, and sizes of items that will go into your project. (Don't settle for general or vague descriptions.) Materials may be difficult to match for size, color, or style and will cost accordingly. You are unlikely to make all of your product selections this early in the process. But you should have a general idea of what you want, so you can tell if your remodeler's allowances are realistic in view of your lifestyle. If they aren't, you will have to make up the difference later.

Contract specifications often contain some or all of the information listed below.

Site Preparation. If fences and other landscaping elements block access to the site, determine who is obligated to remove and replace them. Who is responsible for cutting and removing trees standing on the site of your proposed project?

Excavating and Grading. If your project involves an addition, who will pay the cost of hauling away and/or disposing of excess dirt and rock, if necessary? Who is responsible for any finish grading, sodding, and/or landscaping around the new structure?

Concrete and Masonry. The plans will show footings for walls, fireplaces, chimneys, garage floors, piers, walkways, driveways, and patios. Specifications might include such details as the face of a fireplace, firebox size, lining, hearth material, hearth extension, and style of mantel or surround.

Windows, Doors, and Skylights. Specifications list these items according to manufacturer, style, sizes, quantity, options, color, and any site modifications required, such as special moldings.

Thermal and Moisture Protection. This section specifies such items as insulation to walls, ceilings, floors, roof, and the foundation, along with the manufacturer, the thickness, and the R-value. It also describes the roofing material and its manufacturer, weight, color, nailing pattern, and roofing paper. This section also identifies the appropriate ventilation (including fans), whether roof, soffit, and/or ridge vents.

Interior Carpentry. Your remodeler should spell out the species and grade of lumber for all interior trim, including moldings, base, closet shelving, stairway treads, risers, handrails, and newel posts.

Exterior Carpentry. If you're making improvements to the exterior of your home, your specifications should include details on trim, moldings and casings, siding, fascias, soffits, and decks.

Cabinets. If precise products cannot be specified at this time, your remodeler should provide realistic allowances for kitchen cabinets, vanities, countertops, bookcases, and entertainment centers.

Ceilings and Floors. This section describes any ceiling treatments such as smooth or sand finish, drop or acoustical, cathedral, vaulted, or other design. Your remodeler will specify your flooring choices by room—carpet, tile, vinyl, hardwood.

Ceramic Tile. If you're planning to use ceramic tile in your project, your remodeler should specify the manufacturer, style number, size, color, grout color, and thresholds.

Painting. These specifications should include the manufacturer, color, finish, number of coats, preparation, and method of application for any rooms or exterior surfaces affected by your project.

Plumbing. Your contract should specify such details as piping and fittings, number of lavatories, shower or shower/tub units, special overflow pans (for any shower on an upper floor), outside faucets and locations, washer-dryer connections, basins, and faucets.

Heating, Ventilation, Air-Conditioning, and Solar Heat. Your remodeler should specify the number of zones, thermostats, locations of compressors for air-conditioning units, location of heating and cooling ducts, and the manufacturer and model number of any furnace, boiler, or air-conditioning unit installed, along with the energy source.

Electrical. In a remodeling project involving multiple rooms, your electrical needs may be specified on a room-by-room basis. For smaller projects your remodeler may simply list the number of outlets required by code and any additional ones you request, along with known lighting fixtures, their manufacturer, model number, style, and color. Schedule an early walk-through with your remodeler, electrical contractor, or lighting designer to determine where you want switches, speakers, and fixtures. If your project involves extensive electrical work and specialized fixtures, you may want to incorporate an electrical plan into the contract documents.

Appliances. If appliances are included in the contract price, your remodeler should specify the manufacturer, model number, style, color, options, and who is responsible for removing any old appliances and installing the new ones.

Change Orders

As detailed and thorough as you and your remodeler have been during the planning stages, you're bound to encounter a need—or wish—for changes during the course of your project. Some minor changes will not affect the overall cost of the job; other complex changes may involve substantial cost increases.

Change orders prevent misunderstandings, leave nothing to the imagination, and help prevent project costs from getting out of control. Remodelers use change order forms specifically for these purposes (Figure 5-1). Regardless of the scope of work involved in the change and no matter how comfortable you feel with your remodeler, protect your investment in the project and the relationship by always specifying any changes in writing. Memories can vary or fade, and disagreements can crop up. Be careful of your own behavior because the temptation to give changes orally can be really strong.

Sometimes change orders clarify a given selection or product decision. Some remodelers use change orders when a pending decision becomes an actual decision, such as when you chose your roof color.

Before you deviate from your original plans, find out how the change will affect the total job. For example, adding a cooking island and wet bar to my kitchen remodeling plans seemed fairly straightforward until I started to factor in the additional costs of plumbing, ductwork, appliances, cabinets, and labor. Any time you add a window or door, you are not just buying another unit. You must also pay for framing, installing, trimming, and painting that window or door.

> *On any major home improvement project, it is not unusual for changes from the contract plans to occur as construction progresses. Try to keep changes to a minimum. However, when they are necessary, put them in writing signed by both you and the contractor. Usually additional cost [is] involved, and this should be covered in the change order to avoid surprises later on.*
>
> —A. Michael Marino, President, Better Business Bureau of Rhode Island, Warwick, Rhode Island

You should also ask whether your changes will delay the completion date. If you order a downdraft cooktop after installation of your cooking island, the 6 to 8 weeks it takes to arrive could substantially delay your project.

Your remodeler will assign a number to each change order in incorporating them into the original contract. Expect all change orders to be payable when the work is agreed to or at the next regularly scheduled payment. Discuss the terms with your remodeler.

A standard change order will include some or all of the following clauses.

Job Reference Information. Each change order should reference the original job name, location, phone number, date of contract, and homeowners' names.

Figure 5-1. Sample Change Order

[Use a change order for any deviation from the contract.]

CHANGE ORDER

From: _____

_____

_____

To: _____

_____

_____

Number _____

PHONE	DATE
JOB NAME/LOCATION	
JOB NUMBER	JOB PHONE
EXISTING CONTRACT NO.	DATE OF EXISTING CONTRACT

We hereby agree to make the change(s) specified below:

>

>

Payment for this Change Order is due upon completion of the change order work. The estimated completion date provided for in paragraph _____ of the contract is now _____ .
date

NOTE: This Change Order becomes part of and in conformance with the existing contract.

WE AGREE hereby to make the change(s) specified above at this price ⇨	$	
DATE	PREVIOUS CONTRACT AMOUNT	$
AUTHORIZED SIGNATURE (CONTRACTOR)	REVISED CONTRACT TOTAL	$

ACCEPTED — The above prices and specifications of this Change Order are satisfactory and are hereby accepted. All work to be performed under same terms and conditions as specified in original contract unless otherwise stipulated.

Date of acceptance _____

Signature _____
(OWNER)

Source: Adapted with permission from Matt Davitt, Davitt Woodworks, Inc., North Kingstown, Rhode Island

Description of Work. All change orders should include a complete, accurate, and detailed description of the work to be performed.

Extension of Completion Date. If the work affects the completion date, the change order should specify the new completion date.

Payment Terms. The contract should include terms for payment of the change orders. However the terms may be preprinted or spelled out again on each change order.

Signatures. The owner or a designated owner and the remodeler must sign all change orders.

Lien Releases

This signed list of remodelers, subcontractors, vendors, and suppliers who provide labor and/or materials for your project, states that they waive their right to place a lien on your property. Lien releases will protect you if your remodeler defaults on the financial obligations to subcontractors and suppliers associated with your project. State law determines who is entitled to a lien. It usually extends to first-tier subcontractors and suppliers who can establish that they supplied products that were used in the project. Liens cloud your title, make it difficult to sell your property, and are difficult and costly to remove. Removal of the lien requires payment of the disputed amount or a court decision.

Think of a lien release or lien waiver form as a receipt for payment for all the products and services that have gone into your project. You may encounter several types of lien waiver forms. The long form (Figure 5-2) combines materials and services and provides space for several signatures and the amounts of the payments made. The short form individually acknowledges each cash disbursement to each subcontractor or supplier.

Legal Advice

You may want to have your attorney look over the contract, but avoid getting bogged down in protracted, back-and-forth sessions haggling over details. You could end up spending nearly as much on attorney's fees as you do on the remodeling job.

You are almost ready to begin the physical alterations to your property. Take some time now to anticipate the impact your project will have on your immediate surroundings, your lifestyle, and your emotional well-being.

Figure 5-2. Sample Final Lien Release

In consideration of the amounts listed that have been previously paid to us by _____ _____ or for other valuable consideration, we the undersigned do hereby sever-ally release all liens that we respectively have or may have upon said premises for services rendered or to be rendered, or for materials furnished or to be furnished in the erection, construction, or repair of building on said premises: _____

_____ $ _____		_____ $ _____
General Contractor		Insulation
_____ $ _____		_____ $ _____
Architect		Iron and Steel
_____ $ _____		_____ $ _____
Framing		Kitchen Cabinets
_____ $ _____		_____ $ _____
Electrician		Lumber Dealer
_____ $ _____		_____ $ _____
Excavating, Cellar, ISDS* and Stone for same		Mason
_____ $ _____		_____ $ _____
Laying Floor		Painter
_____ $ _____		_____ $ _____
Foundation		Plasterer
_____ $ _____		_____ $ _____
Grading		Plumber
_____ $ _____		_____ $ _____
Heating Contractor		Concrete
_____ $ _____		
Finish Labor		

_____
*Individual sewage disposal system.

Source: Adapted with permission from Matt Davitt, Davitt Woodworks, Inc., North Kingstown, Rhode Island.

Chapter 6

From Permits to Packing and Preparation

You have obtained financing or applied for it, you're working with your remodeler on design, and you have signed a remodeling contract. Before the job begins, you must acquire the necessary permits. Some permits can take weeks—or even months—to obtain. While the process can be time-consuming and laborious, those permits protect the safety and welfare of individuals, preserve the environment, and honor the legal rights of your neighbors or the owners of property that abuts yours.

Responsibility for Obtaining Permits

Many remodelers prefer to handle the permitting process themselves. They understand the procedure better than the homeowner, and they can get through the paperwork quicker. However, if your remodeler agrees to handle the permitting, you should know which permits your project requires because ultimately you are the responsible party. This knowledge can prevent lengthy delays and even stiff fines for noncompliance. Certain permits can be expensive if you must hire an engineer, attorney, remodeler, or other professional to assist you in the application process. Normally your remodeler or the subcontractor doing the work is responsible for obtaining electrical, plumbing, and mechanical permits. Projects that involve updating or facelifting within the existing footprint of your house usually require fewer permits than those that alter the overall dimensions. Contact your local building inspector's office as soon as possible to determine which permits you need. In dealing with the people who process your applications, remember that they may not have the leeway to make exceptions because their jobs are defined by law.

Types of Permits and Approvals

Before obtaining a building permit, you first must satisfy all the regulatory bodies that govern your property. The required permits for each project vary and are obtained in different ways, but some permits are fairly common in remodeling (Figure 6-1).

Figure 6-1. Permits for Remodeling

[Avoid construction delays and fines. Contact your local building inspector's office before beginning any remodeling project to determine which permits your municipality and state require. Use this checklist to track the permits necessary for your job, such as building, environmental, septic system, demolition, archaeological, historic, and zoning. Copy this form onto index cards.]

Type of permit _____

Name of permitting office _____

Location _____

Phone number _____

Contact person_____

Processing time _____

Expiration date_____

Fees $_____

Supporting documents required _____

_____

Building Permit

A building permit from your local permitting office, prominently displayed at the site, indicates that you have complied with the regulations governing the application process, obtained all ancillary permits, paid all necessary fees, and received the green light to proceed with your project.

Historic Permit

If the property you are remodeling is in a historic district, you may have to obtain a separate permit from the local historic preservation society or fine arts commission.

Zoning Approval

Learn your property-line setbacks before you start designing your project. You may need approval from the zoning board if your addition or new structure doesn't conform to existing property-line setbacks. (Setbacks are the distances from your front, rear, and side property lines in which you may not build anything.) Some jurisdictions also impose height restrictions on new homes and additions. You need to find out if any of these conditions apply to your project.

Applying for a zoning variance (permission to override an existing regulation) can be time-consuming and frustrating. You could spend months preparing and presenting your project to your local zoning board. However, if you believe your request is reasonable, don't be dissuaded from applying for a variance.

Be sure you're working on your own property. You don't want to find out after the concrete has been poured for the foundation that the structure is encroaching on someone else's land. Don't take chances. If you have any doubts, have a land survey done to reaffirm your property boundaries and avoid encroachments.

Coastal or Other Environmental Approvals

If the property you intend to improve lies close to an ocean, freshwater pond, stream, or wetlands, expect your project to undergo rigorous scrutiny by the coastal authority or department of environmental management or protection in your state. Often tedious and drawn out, the permitting process attempts to balance environmental concerns with the rights of the homeowner.

Septic System Approval

If your property is served by an individual septic system rather than a sewer, the department of environmental management or similar agency may require you to demonstrate that the planned improvements will not put extra strain on your existing septic system. For example, if your blueprints indicate that you are planning to add one or more bedrooms to your home, the regulatory agency in your state may ask you to enlarge your septic system. You also may have to upgrade your septic system if the area of your project exceeds a certain percentage of the total square footage.

Fees

Most permitting agencies charge the homeowner or the remodeler a nonrefundable fee at the time of application. Rates vary. The fee for a building permit is often based on a percentage of the contract price while some state agencies, such as a department of environmental management or protection, may charge a flat fee for a permit. You also may have to hire professionals to prepare the supporting documents for your application. For example, the application fee for a septic system permit in Rhode Island is only $100, but I've paid hundreds of dollars more to hire a civil engineer to design my septic system.

The Preconstruction Meeting

The preconstruction meeting is an opportunity for you and your remodeler to discuss all the guidelines and rules for your project. The more information you can convey early on, the less chance of misunderstandings and unfulfilled expectations later. Use the worksheet in Figure 6-2 as a guide for this important discussion.

Kelley Hale, president of Hale Remodeling, Inc., in El Cerrito, California, uses the preconstruction meeting to let homeowners know that they can expect some

Figure 6-2. The Preconstruction Meeting

[A successful remodeling project requires mutual cooperation between you and your family and the whole remodeling crew. Use this worksheet to help define your expectations and reduce confusion.]

❏ **Designated Spokespeople**. Who has the authority to make day-to-day decisions, change the scope of work, initiate change orders, and so on? _____
In case of an after-hours emergency, whom should you call? _____

❏ **Furniture Removal**. Who is responsible for removing your furniture and other belongings and then returning them to the remodeled space? Will you need to rent warehouse storage space? _____

❏ **Smoking**. Is smoking permitted? ❏ Yes ❏ No If so, where? _____

❏ **Phone Use**. Is use of your phone allowed? ❏ Yes ❏ No If so, will you allow personal calls, only business calls, or calls made with a worker's calling card? (You can also have your phone company block long distance calls on your phone.) _____

❏ **Use of the Bathroom**. If you have more than one usable bathroom available, will you designate one of them for your remodeler's crew and subcontractors to use? ❏ Yes ❏ No (Present your expectations for the daily clean-up of this room and any other common areas in writing.) _____

❏ **Safety**. What safety precautions will your remodeler take? _____
_____ Does your remodeler know where to find and how to use the fire extinguishers in your home? ❏ Yes ❏ No

❏ **Dust Containment**. What abatement techniques will your remodeler use? (Also discuss with the remodeler what government regulations require. Even the tiniest amounts of horsehair plaster, insulation, and asbestos found in old houses are unsafe to breathe.)
_____

❏ **Parking**. Where are construction workers allowed to park their vehicles in relationship to your vehicles, neighbors' vehicles, landscaping, and the like? (In areas with little or no off-street parking, parking one extra vehicle could be a challenge. In such a case, parking concerns would become a central issue in the preconstruction meeting.) _____
_____

❏ **Language**. Have you specifically requested that your remodeler's crew and subcontractors respect your preference for profanity-free speech at all times? ❏ Yes ❏ No

❏ **Radios**. Will you mind if workers listen to a radio? ❏ Yes ❏ No At what volume? (If you work at home or have children who take daily naps, you may want to discuss ways to protect sound-sensitive spaces such as their bedrooms and your office.) _____

❏ **Pets**. Do your pets require any special considerations? ❏ Yes ❏ No Will you allow workers to bring pets onto your project? ❏ Yes ❏ No If so, put any restricted areas in writing. (Many remodelers prohibit this practice.)_____
_____

(Continued)

Figure 6-2. The Preconstruction Meeting (Continued)

❏ **Start and Stop Times**. What time will workers begin and stop work at your home? Start _____ Stop _____

❏ **Security.** Will workers need a key for entry, or will a family member be home to open the door? _____
If you work outside the home and will arrive after the crew has left for the day, what procedure do you want followed for lock-up? _____
Who is responsible for closing any windows opened during the day? _____

❏ **Jobsite Signage.** Will you allow your remodeler and subcontractors to erect their marketing signs on your property? ❏ Yes ❏ No If so, where and for how long? _____
_____

❏ **Storage.** Where will your remodeler store building materials before installation? _____
_____
Do you have any security concerns you want addressed and preventive measures taken?
_____

❏ **Debris.** Where will your remodeler locate the dumpster or waste bin on the property? _____
_____ Can you use it for trash unrelated to the remodeling contract (for example, if you decide to clean out your garage or attic while your project is under way)? ❏ Yes ❏ No

❏ **Salvaging Materials.** Would you like to save any special objects from the demolition, such as antique lighting fixtures, a door, or cabinets? ❏ Yes ❏ No If not, will you mind if the remodeler's crew or the subcontractors remove any discarded items for personal use? ❏ Yes ❏ No

❏ **Children.** If you have young children, have you discussed childproofing the area with your remodeler? ❏ Yes ❏ No (Children should not be left unsupervised at home during a remodeling project. A remodeling worksite is a congested, dangerous place. If your children are often home alone, perhaps you could arrange for them to visit after school with a supervised friend.) _____
Have you pointed out the speed limit in your neighborhood (especially if small children are around) and stated your expectations that everyone associated with your project will obey traffic laws in your community? ❏ Yes ❏ No

❏ **Delivery Routes.** Have you established delivery routes that minimize disturbance to outside structures, plants, shrubs, and flower beds? ❏ Yes ❏ No (Construction vehicles such as concrete trucks and drywall boom trucks can wreck landscaping if you haven't planned ahead.) _____

❏ **Visitors.** Do you mind if crew members and subcontractors have visitors, such as spouses and friends, while working on your job? ❏ Yes ❏ No _____

❏ **Communication Center**. Where will you set up the project's communication center? If it's in a master bedroom, study, or other private area, who will you allow to enter this area? _____

(Continued)

Figure 6-2. The Preconstruction Meeting (Continued)

❏ **Makeshift Stations**. Will you allow workers to use your appliances to refrigerate and heat up their food? ❏ Yes ❏ No (Delineate the workers' space and the household's space and change these as the job progresses.) _____

❏ **Power Interruptions.** Does your remodeler anticipate any power interruptions during the project? ❏ Yes ❏ No What special provisions must be made for refrigerators, computers, fax machines, timepieces, and the like? _____

❏ **Clean-Up.** Can areas be simply swept? ❏ Yes ❏ No Or will you require a complete cleaning job every day so you can use the space? ❏ Yes ❏ No _____

❏ **Open Houses**. Will you allow your remodeler to bring prospects through your home? ❏ Yes ❏ No With your special permission only? ❏ Yes ❏ No Do you prefer to be present? ❏ Yes ❏ No

---

stress, but he presents the issue in a gentle, humorous way. Hale wrote a "Remodeling Blues" letter to ease homeowners' concerns (Figure 6-3).

Your project should continue with regular weekly meetings between you and your remodeler or his or her representative. How will critical information be communicated? Some remodelers use a daily log of questions and comments between the customer and the lead carpenter or other person in charge of the job. This log is usually a notebook, anchored to prevent accidental removal or loss. Daily comments or questions are added by the customer and the remodeler's representative, but this log is not a substitute for regular meetings.

I establish a private, secure "communication center" in the master bedroom, home office, or some other area to which only I and the remodeler's representative have access. This way, if I have a problem with a subcontractor or crew member, I can leave a discreet message for management's eyes only. Change orders, checks, and other important papers can also be left here.

Schedule

Ask your remodeler to provide you with a rough work schedule for your project and the dates by which you must make your product decisions and other selections (Figure 6-4). Find out which decisions require the longest lead time. For example, some kitchen cabinets could take as long as 6 to 8 weeks to arrive, and custom cabinets could take even longer.

Plan ahead, and you won't feel overwhelmed and pressured into making poor decisions about your project. Planning ahead will take the pressure off you and allow the project to proceed on time.

Move Temporarily or Stay Put

Depending on the scope of work, you and your family may want to move out of your home temporarily during the project. If you vacate the premises, your

Figure 6-3. "Remodeling Blues" Letter

Dear Homeowner,

Remodeling is an ordeal. It is like having a woodworking shop located inside your house. It means taking your house apart in order to put it back together again, only differently. All the while, your home is a workplace to a dozen strangers.

The purpose of this letter is not to frighten you away from your project, but to prepare you for the stress you will inevitably feel. Every remodeling job creates some amount of disorder, dirt, and confusion. Privacy may seem a thing of the past. Your house might feel more like a bus station with inspectors, subcontractors, and crew members coming and going. We will work hard to help you maintain your comfort and privacy despite these conditions. Our employees understand that this is not just a worksite, it is your home.

Remodeling proceeds in stages and some of these are more difficult than others. Chances are you've already gone through the first stage, the inevitable delays and frustrations that come in dealing with planning departments to secure permits and zoning variances.

The next stress cycle comes with the demolition phase of your project. At this point, you see your house, your chief asset, crumbling around you. Electrical, plumbing, or heating service may be temporarily interrupted. The house may seem cold if the siding has to be removed on an exterior wall. You know you are paying for all this and start to wonder whether anything that looks so bad will ever look good again. All we can tell you at this point is that you will see progress every day. Once we start framing, your project will begin to take form.

Meanwhile, dust has an amazing ability to penetrate even the tiniest cracks and holes. We'll do our best to keep this to a minimum by sealing up any penetrations and keeping the jobsite neat. But some dust is an inevitable part of the process.

After the major structural work is completed, the job seems to slow down as your house is invaded by a new group of people: subcontractors and inspectors. The work at this step has become more detailed and less impressive. But it is one of the most important stages. So hang in there because the next phase, when the drywall is installed, is one of the most exciting (despite a layer of fine, white dust that seems to be everywhere).

The last and often the longest stage is the finish work. The steps involved at this phase make for very slight daily changes. Rest assured we are working! We'll do the best we can to meet any deadlines you've set for us, but our original schedule is based on our bid. Anything that happens along the way, including back-ordered materials or change orders, will cause delays.

Finally the day comes when you can begin using the space as you intended. We may be back on the scene to do a few little jobs that remain, but you can breathe a sigh of relief—you've survived the worst of it.

Sincerely,

Kelley Hale

Source: Reprinted with permission from Kelley Hale, Hale Remodeling, El Cerrito, California.

Figure 6-4. Sample Work Schedule

[Ask your remodeler to give you a work schedule for your project, so you can keep up with choosing products and other important decisions.]

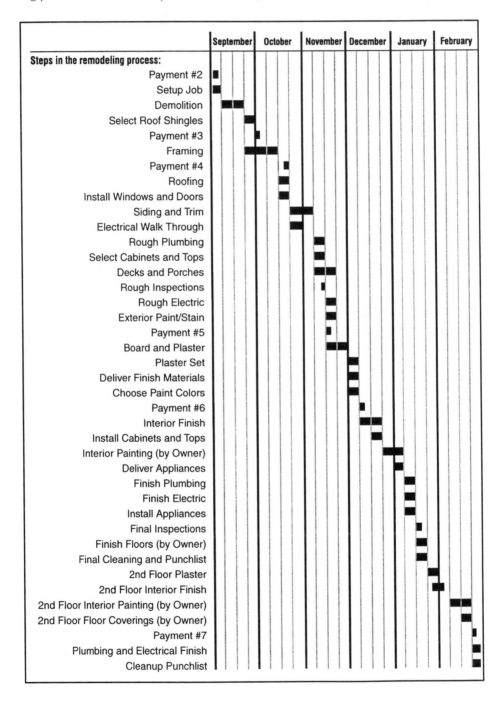

Source: Adapted with permission from Matt Davitt, President, Davitt Woodworks, Inc., North Kingstown, Rhode Island

remodeler may finish your project more quickly because he or she won't need to do a major clean-up each night. Of course, each situation is unique, and your decision to move or stay in the house will depend on several factors.

Size of Household. A single person or a couple with no children at home might find remaining in a home being remodeled easier than would a couple with children. Practically speaking, a couple with children might find dining out more complicated.

Budgetary Constraints. Taking on another housing expense for monthly rent may not be financially feasible for some homeowners. Perhaps you could factor your relocation expenses into the overall financing of the project. Would a friend or family member living nearby be willing to put you and your family up temporarily? When considering this option, be aware that sometimes the solution can be worse than the problem.

Scope of Work. Even a single-room conversion can turn a household upside down if the scope of work is extensive. You must analyze that room's importance to your household and determine what impact the suspension of its functions will have while your project is going on.

Duration of Project. If the project is expected to take only a few weeks, most people can put up with the disruption. More complex, whole-house remodeling projects and several simultaneous additions often necessitate greater sacrifice and the need for carefully planned substitutions for interrupted services.

At the time we sign the contract, we have an informal discussion with the homeowners about what to expect. Our goal is always to align expectations with reality. The facts are that remodeling is a dirty, invasive business. We brace homeowners by lowering their expectations for the process. We then exceed their visions by trying hard to be thoroughly clean and meticulous. For example, we protect all door openings and install fans in the windows creating negative draft—drawing the dust outside. Exceeding expectations makes for satisfied customers.

—Bill Asdal, Partner, Asdal and Company—Builders, LLC*, Chester, New Jersey

Capacity for Makeshift Spaces. Make a list of all things you may take for granted—such as hot water, a flushable toilet, cold beverages, a hot meal, a clean bed—then determine which basic services will be interrupted by your project. Can you create makeshift spaces or substitutes for crucial services? Could you find room for a small refrigerator and microwave oven next to the bathroom when a kitchen is out of commission (Figure 6-5)? If not, you might want to live elsewhere for a time or at least consider going elsewhere for food, hygiene, and respite.

Weather Conditions. If you are planning to remove the roof in an area of the country prone to periods of uncertain weather, you may need temporary housing, at least until the house is weathertight again.

---

*Limited liability corporation.

Figure 6-5. Makeshift Kitchen

Make your life a little more manageable during a kitchen remodeling project by assembling a makeshift kitchen. A hot beverage or bowl of soup can make a big difference in your outlook. The coffeemaker in this makeshift kitchen is on wheels and can be moved to allow access to the small refrigerator and microwave oven.

Photo by the author

Packing, Storing, and Preparation

One of the least enjoyable tasks in any remodeling project is the packing and storing of personal effects such as furniture, clothing, and kitchenware. Unfortunately your cherished possessions can get in the way of a remodeling project, so arrange to remove them. I've used my remodeling projects as opportunities to clean house and dispose of unnecessary belongings. Anticipate the rooms and areas your project will affect and take the necessary steps to remove, store, or cover your things. When you are packing, look beyond just the space being remodeled. Your remodeler may need access to spaces that aren't being changed, such as the basement, attic, or garage, as well as the driveway or the grounds (Figure 6-6).

General Living Quarters. Again, who will move and, if necessary, store your furniture and personal belongings? How will unmoved items be protected? Your whole house is likely to feel the effects of a remodeling job. Fragile items should be removed from the workpath.

Figure 6-6. Packing Guidelines

[Protect your belongings by preparing the spaces to which your remodeler will need access. Circle all the belongings that must be moved and indicate how and where you intend to move them. Check each room or area as you complete it.]

❑ **Kitchen.** Pots and pans, dishes, glassware, silverware, dry goods, perishables, cleaning, supplies, small appliances, rugs, plants, wall hangings, light fixtures, other _____

❑ **Bathroom.** Paper goods, toiletries, towels, rugs, plants, wall hangings, light fixtures, cleaning supplies, other _____

❑ **Closets.** Clothing, footwear, accessories, blankets, linens, other _____

❑ **Home office.** Books, furniture, rugs, plants, wall hangings, light fixtures, files shelving, storage equipment, electronic equipment, other_____

❑ **Garage.** Vehicles, tools, bicycles, lawn and sports equipment, other _____

❑ **Attic.** Storage boxes, shelving, furniture, luggage, holiday decorations, other _____

❑ **Basement.** Tools, storage boxes, appliances, toys, furniture, exercise equipment, household supplies, other _____

❑ **Bedrooms.** Furniture, rugs, plants, wall hangings, light fixtures, accessories, jewelry other _____

❑ **Living room.** Furniture, rugs, plants, wall hangings, light fixtures, accessories, books, other_____

If your remodeling project necessitates removing your furniture and other personal belongings from your home, consider several factors before storing them. According to Kevin Kernan, owner of Consumers' Moving Co., Inc., in Cranston, Rhode Island, "The best way to store furniture is in a clean, dry, heated, and alarmed warehouse. You should avoid unheated, ministorage-type facilities with concrete floors. Moisture can cause mold and mildew. Cold temperatures can cause glued joints to dry out and certain woods to actually change colors. For the utmost in protection, blanket-wrap all furniture and stretch-wrap all upholstery in plastic."

Basement. Your remodeler may need access to your basement to hook into your electrical service and water- and wastelines and—in the case of an addition— to tie into the existing foundation.

Attic. Even if your project doesn't involve opening your roof, your remodeler may need a passageway into your attic to accommodate vent pipes and electrical wiring.

Garage. If your remodeler needs to store building materials in your garage, you may have to move garbage cans, strollers, yard tools, bicycles, and other frequently used items to another, more accessible place in your home.

Driveway. Do you need to temporarily relocate campers, trailers, unregistered motor vehicles, and the like to accommodate workers' vehicles? Should you restrict heavy trucks from using your driveway? (Many driveways are not designed to support them?)

Grounds. Anticipate the effect delivery vehicles, heavy equipment, dumpsters, and concrete trucks will have on the grounds of your house, including your landscaping, fencing, patios, picnic tables, and other lawn furniture.

Activity Curve

Homeowners experience all kinds of emotions during a remodeling project. From anticipation to euphoria, emotions generally follow the activity curve of the job. For example, my expectations are usually the highest when I'm planning the project with my designer. Once carpenters, electricians, and other subcontractors descend upon my home, I expect to feel some degree of uneasiness. However, as the project begins to wind down and I prepare to take my space back, my emotional pendulum swings in the other direction again.

A remodeling project can affect more than the rooms of your house. It can also upset the daily balance of your life and cause anxiety, stress, and feelings of loss of control. Some people experience a natural phenomenon known as remodeling fever when they feel that their personal space has been invaded. For them, the nesting instinct is strong, and it compels them to protect their environment (in this case, their homes), their loved ones, and their personal belongings.

The best way to deal with remodeling fever is to prepare for the inevitable disruptions and realize that these changes are only temporary (Figure 6-7).

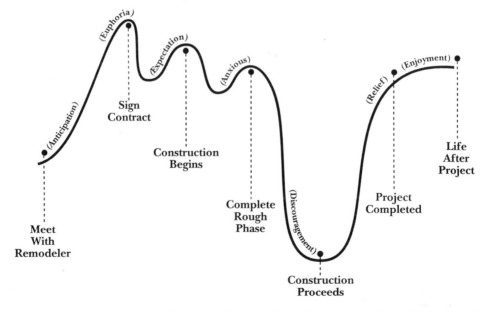

Source: Reprinted with permission from Cindy Kamens, Cindy Kamens Graphics, Terryville, Connecticut

Figure 6-7. Activity Curve

Being aware of the various stages of a remodeling project can help prepare you for the inevitable mood swings you will experience during the life of the project.

An Antidote for Remodeling Fever

You can counteract remodeling fever by planning celebrations for certain phases of the project. For example, plan a dinner for your family in your newly remodeled kitchen or dining room once the space is plastered or the drywall taping and spackling is finished. Even if the food is take-out, a little merrymaking will go a long way toward lessening the stress of the project. One night after our new family room was plastered, we brought in a few pieces of furniture, made some popcorn, ran an extension cord for the portable television, and watched a video.

The best and simplest advice comes from New Jersey remodeler Bill Asdal, who says, "Remodeling your home is a finite experience; it is not going to last forever. At some point, it will be over."

Stress comes in waves, depending on the stage of the job. By anticipating the stress points you can prepare yourself.

—Kelley Hale, Hale Remodeling, Inc., El Cerrito, California

Chapter 7

From Foundations to Finishes

If your head is swimming with all kinds of new terms, such as *dado* and *sheathing*, you may not believe that remodeling is a fairly straightforward process. This chapter will walk you through many of the tasks in that process—from preparing the site to finishing the floors. The worksheet in Figure 7-1 will help you brainstorm ideas for eight of the most common remodeling projects: kitchen, bath, bedroom, garage, attic, addition, deck, and basement. The checklist in Figure 7-2 will guide you through the total remodeling process.

Tasks in the Remodeling Process

While most remodelers are prepared for the unexpected (and you should be too), remodeling projects usually follow a fairly systematic, routine chain of events. Remodelers call this the critical path, and each stage in the process builds on a previous required activity. For example, the remodeler cannot insulate walls, ceilings, and floors until the rough plumbing, heating, and electrical work have been completed.

The tasks in a typical critical path are discussed in the paragraphs that follow. The other decisions you'll need to make when each task begins appear in parentheses.

Prepare the Site

Site preparation involves the moving and/or removal of fences, structures, landscaping, vehicles, and other impediments to the project's workpath, footprint, and surrounding areas. Be sure to arrange for someone to transplant shrubs and flower beds and protect trees (Figure 7-3). If your project involves an addition, your remodeler will clear and grub areas around it and stake out the new structure. (You also need to select and order windows, doors, and skylights.)

Excavate, Grade, and Prepare the Foundation

Excavation removes earth to a depth and width large enough to accept the foundation for your new structure. Your excavation contractor will—

- dig the hole
- form footings
- form and pour the foundation
- strip forms
- waterproof and insulate the foundation
- treat for pests
- backfill and rough grade

Figure 7-1. Brainstorm Ideas

[Use this worksheet to clarify your remodeling goals and study the possibilities. Ask yourself a lot of questions when planning your project and consult your remodeler for specific advice on each of these ideas.]

❏ **Remodeling a Kitchen.** What are you trying to accomplish? Add space? Redesign the existing area? Change the style? Update? Facelift? _____

_____

_____

❏ **Remodeling a Bath.** What are you trying to accomplish? Add space? Redesign the existing area? Change the style? Update? Facelift? _____

_____

_____

❏ **Remodeling a Bedroom.** What are you trying to accomplish? Add space? Redesign the existing area? Change the style? _____

_____

_____

❏ **Adding a Garage.** How many vehicles will you park in the garage? (A typical two-car garage measures 24 by 24 feet.) Do recreational vehicles such as boats, campers, jet skis, and snowmobiles also require storage? Will you use the garage to store tools, supplies, or sporting goods? Will you attach the garage to your home, or will you locate it elsewhere on your property? If attached, how will you connect the two—with an overhang, covered walkway, or enclosed space? Will the pedestrian entry into the house change? Would you like living space above the garage? If so, how will you gain access to it? What type of garage door will you use? Are you planning any decorative touches, such as a weather vane?_____

_____

_____

❏ **Remodeling an Attic.** Will you use the space as an extra bedroom, home office, entertainment center, exercise room, or family room? Do you want to keep some of the space for storage? How will you heat, cool, and light the space? Will you require dormers, skylights, or windows? Will you use the entire attic in an open floorplan arrangement, or will you divide the space? Will you need to give up part of a room below the attic for

(Continued)

Figure 7-1. Brainstorm Ideas (Continued)

stairway construction? (If you use the attic as a bedroom, one of your windows must be large enough to exit in case of an emergency.) _____

_____

_____

❑ **Building an Addition.** Will you use the space as an extra bedroom, home office, entertainment center, exercise room, or family room? Do you envision a cozy nook or a spacious great room? How will you heat, cool, and light the space? Where will you locate the addition, and how will you enter the new space? Do you want a one- or two-story addition? Will you want the addition built on a full foundation (for a full basement) or on a slab or over a crawl space? _____

_____

_____

❑ **Remodeling or Adding a Deck.** Are you trying to add space? Does an existing deck just need improvement? Will you gain access to the deck from ground level as well as inside the house? Where do you want the stairs? If you want to use the deck for entertaining, how much space do you need to seat your family and friends comfortably? Determine where to place furniture and other accessories, such as barbecue equipment. (You may want to screen in the deck later, so decide now on the approximate placement of windows, doors, and skylights.) _____

_____

_____

❑ **Remodeling a Basement.** Will you use the space for an extra bedroom, home office, entertainment center, exercise room, or family room? How will you heat, cool, and light the space? Will you use the entire basement in an open floorplan arrangement, or will you divide the space? Do you want to keep part of the area for storage? Will you enter the basement from outdoors as well as inside the house? Where will you place furniture and other items? (If your remodeler must move lolly columns to make room for a pool table or other oversized piece of equipment, you may also have to make structural alterations. Your remodeler may need to relocate wires and pipes and enclose them in a chase or feature specially built for this purpose.) Do you need to create a separate utility room for your furnace or boiler, water heater, and washer and dryer? _____

_____

_____

Figure 7-2. Tasks in the Remodeling Process

[Anticipate the major tasks in your remodeling project by using this checklist to monitor progress.]

❏ Brainstorm ideas (see Figure 7-1).

❏ Determine space requirements. Will the footprint remain the same or is expansion necessary? What will be the new dimensions? If you are adding on, make sure your addition conforms to the applicable property-line setbacks and lot coverage constraints.

❏ Decide on the placement of openings such as windows, doors, skylights. Will access to the space change?

❏ Decide what appliances and fixtures will be necessary and their approximate placement.

❏ Draw a rough sketch of the existing plan and the proposed plan.

❏ Determine where to place furniture.

❏ Make a list of needed products and materials.

❏ Find a professional remodeler.

❏ Set up a budget and finance the project.

❏ Design with your budget in mind.

❏ Study and understand all the contract documents.

❏ Obtain permits.

❏ Have a preconstruction meeting.

❏ Pack, move, and store belongings.

❏ Prepare the site.

❏ Excavate and grade.

❏ Form and pour the foundation.

❏ Demolish existing conditions.

❏ Complete rough carpentry.

❏ Apply exterior siding.

❏ Install rough heating, ventilation, and air-conditioning systems.

❏ Install rough plumbing system.

❏ Install rough electrical system.

❏ Inspect all rough work.

❏ Insulate walls, ceilings, and floors.

❏ Inspect insulation.

❏ Install drywall or plaster walls and ceilings.

❏ Prime walls and ceilings.

❏ Finish heating, ventilation, and air-conditioning systems.

❏ Finish carpentry.

❏ Paint, stain, or wallpaper interior walls and trim.

❏ Lay unfinished hardwood floor, tile, and/or vinyl floor covering.

❏ Finish electrical system.

❏ Finish plumbing system.

❏ Sand and finish hardwood floors.

❏ Landscape grounds.

❏ Lay padding and carpeting.

❏ Inspect for certificate of occupancy.

❏ Touch-up paint.

❏ Inspect completed job during homeowner orientation.

❏ Prepare punchlist.

❏ Clean up.

❏ Make final payment.

❏ Understand warranties.

Figure 7-3. Existing Shrubs, Trees, Flower Beds, and Fences

The owners of this property must consider the effect their remodeling plans will have on their shrubs, trees, flower beds, brick walkways, and fences.

(Select shingle color and, if you're planning a fireplace, choose its material. You also need to select kitchen and/or bathroom cabinets, countertops, and appliances. If you plan to repaint your house, choose your interior and exterior paint or stain colors, as well.)

Complete Demolition

Demolition is the removal of existing conditions in the areas slated for remodeling. For me the project usually looks its worse at this point (Figure 7-4), and I'm likely to feel the most vulnerable as I watch part of my home crumbling around me.

Be sure to take special precautions with any areas requiring asbestos or lead removal. Your jurisdiction may require that a specially trained, certified, or licensed contractor remove any asbestos or lead.

Give careful thought to the impact your remodeling plans will have on your existing landscaping. Before construction begins, determine which plantings you would like to save and then decide how you will preserve them during the project. If construction cannot work around the existing plantings, you might consider either incorporating some of the material into plantings already existing on the property or heel them into a temporary holding bed until the construction is over and the material can be safely replanted.

—Martha S. Moore, Landscape Architect, Warren, Rhode Island

Photo by the author

Figure 7-4. Demolition

Workers take a break from the demolition of this oceanfront cottage before beginning reconstruction.

Complete Rough Carpentry

This task involves the construction of the wood skeleton of the structure, including walls, roofs, and floors. Carpenters will—

- set sill plate
- frame deck
- build and stand first-floor walls
- frame second-floor deck (if applicable)
- build and stand second-floor walls
- frame and sheath roof
- run exterior trim
- apply roof shingles and install skylights
- install windows and doors

(If you've chosen to do a walk-through with the remodeler, electrician, or lighting designer, confirm locations for your outlets, switches, and fixtures.)

Apply Exterior Siding

Siding includes the eaves and overhangs, corner boards, the trim around windows and doors, and the actual material applied to your home's exterior to seal it and protect it from the weather.

(You need to select interior paint colors and any specialty moldings such as crown moldings, chair rails, and stair parts.)

Install and Inspect Rough Systems

Subcontractors will install the piping, wiring, and ductwork in your home's walls, floors, and ceilings for heating, ventilation, air-conditioning, plumbing, and electrical systems.

(Select tile and grout colors, vinyl floor coverings, and hardwood floors and finishes.)

Inspections by municipal officials certify that the work performed thus far is safe and meets the building code.

Insulate and Inspect Walls, Ceilings, and Floors

Insulation increases the thermal value of your home by making the house cooler in the summer and warmer in the winter.

Install Drywall or Plaster Walls and Ceilings

Once installed, drywall or plaster helps define the remodeled space and establish the traffic pattern through it. You'll begin to feel now that you're in a real room. Before this task, you could walk between the studs—now you must use the appropriate doorway.

Prime Walls and Ceilings

Priming, the first task in finishing a wall, helps to bond the paint that will come later. If you are planning to wallpaper, your remodeler will apply a special substance to the walls (sizing) to make the wallpaper adhere better.

Finish Heating, Ventilation, and Air-Conditioning

To complete the working systems, subcontractors will connect hardware, fixtures, appliances, and other devices to the rough components.

Finish Carpentry

Finish work is the most visible, detailed, precision-driven, and time-consuming aspect of the project. Finish carpenters will—

- trim out windows
- hang doors and install trim
- install baseboard
- install closet shelving
- hang specialty moldings
- install stair parts
- lay subflooring
- set cabinets and countertops

Paint, Stain, or Wallpaper Interior Walls and Trim

Painting and staining interior walls and trim or wallpapering seals and protects surfaces and begins the decorating process. (Select your carpeting and padding.)

Lay Unfinished Hardwood Floor, Tile, and/or Vinyl Floor Covering

A subcontractor will install the coverings you have chosen over the subfloor.

Finish Electrical System

Electricians will connect appliances, fixtures, and other devices to the rough electrical components. Your electrical contractor will—

◆ connect appliances
◆ hang light fixtures
◆ install light bulbs
◆ tie into the service panel

Finish Plumbing

A subcontractor will connect appliances, fixtures, and other devices to the rough plumbing components and complete the working system. Your plumber will—

◆ connect appliances
◆ set toilets
◆ install faucets
◆ install shower valves and showerheads

The relationship between the code official, the remodeler, and the homeowner need not be an adversarial one. Inspections provide a professional examination of the conditions of your property and give validity to the state of the renovations at that time. Code officials, remodelers, and homeowners all want the same thing—a safe building, free from defects.

—Joseph A. Cirillo, Registered Architect, State Building Commissioner, Providence, Rhode Island

Sand and Finish Hardwood Floors

Sanding removes surface imperfections from wood floors and creates a porous surface for finish materials to penetrate.

Moving On

Now that the whirlwind of project planning, product selection, and actual construction is winding down, can completion be far behind? A few tasks remain before you can reclaim your space, so stay focused as you move on to the final days of your project.

Chapter 8

From Clean-Up to Completion Certificates

One day you'll walk into your new space expecting the usual bustle and notice a strange stillness. All the workers who have been your companions for weeks, maybe even months, have been replaced by a lone carpenter or subcontractor doing last-minute finish or touch-up work. The end of your project is in sight at last, and you're ready to begin final inspections and decorating. But before you can start hanging pictures and curtains and moving your furniture and other belongings back, you need to attend to a few details.

The Remaining Tasks

Landscape the Grounds

While the last flurry of activity is taking place inside your home, the outside of your property is undergoing a transformation of its own. With the long-awaited departure of delivery trucks, construction vehicles, and steady stream of workers, you can finally add the finishing touches to your property. If necessary, subcontractors can hang gutters and shutters to match the new exterior.

Many homeowners prefer to complete their landscaping in stages so they can budget the cost over several years. Depending on the kind of landscaping you have chosen, your remodeler or landscape architect may perform some or all of these jobs:

◆ finish grading
◆ York rake (a mechanical process done with a special rake attached to a tractor, which gathers all the rocks, debris, and branches that have been left on newly turned ground)
◆ dump, spread, and hand-rake loam
◆ lay out beds for flowers, shrubs, and other plants
◆ plant lawns, flowers, shrubs, trees, herbs, and vegetables
◆ install brick walkways, driveways, and edgings around driveways and flower beds and gardens
◆ fertilize the lawn
◆ erect special structures such as gazebos and arbors

A well-landscaped project can be enjoyed from both the interior and the exterior of the house. Too many homeowners overlook landscaping because they don't perceive it as part of the interior space. Actually, landscaping should be reciprocal. I like to take into account both the view I have looking out of the room as well as the one I have looking in from the outside.

Lay Padding and Carpeting

If your project calls for carpeting, your remodeler will schedule installation for one of the last days of the project. No remodeler wants to see new carpeting damaged, so by the time the carpet installers arrive, all other subcontractors and crew members will have either packed up their gear and left or will be working in another area of the house. Carpeting often signals a significant swing in my emotional pendulum.

Before installation, walk through the area to be carpeted to check for annoying squeaks in the floor. The remodeler can easily correct this problem at this stage by putting a few extra fasteners in the subfloor.

Inspect for Certificate of Occupancy

When all the work is completed, your remodeler will notify the building inspector's office that your project is ready for final inspections. In some locations one official makes all of the inspections; other jurisdictions have separate inspectors for electrical, plumbing, and mechanical systems. An inspector can issue citations for code violations that range from the trivial (a missing light bulb in an outside light fixture) to more serious violations (a faulty smoke detector or a chimney with insufficient roof clearance). Although you may want quick correction of any code violations, you may not necessarily be inconvenienced because you are already living in the house.

Touch-Up Paint

Touch-up painting can take several days because of the extensive preparation needed. On the first day, your painter will apply joint compound or spackle to the blemish and allow it to dry overnight or longer. He or she will sand and prime the area the next day or later. The actual painting will occur on yet another day.

Homeowner Orientation

Give yourself ample time to thoroughly inspect the project. If possible, I try to inspect the project several times—once in natural light and once under the artificial lighting that I plan to use. Different lighting often reveals different imperfections. I use a punchlist to keep track of any deficiencies in the quality of the work or materials. A punchlist is a simple form that helps you isolate and evaluate particular tasks and components of your job (Figure 8-1). Use of a punchlist prompts you to ask questions: Is anything missing, such as switch plates or light fixtures? Are any tasks incomplete? Do painted or stained areas feel smooth to the touch?

If you view this inspection as an opportunity to contribute vital quality control to your remodeler, not as a witch-hunt for reasons to complain, you'll be much

Figure 8-1. Kitchen Punchlist

[Use punchlists to guide your final inspection of the work. Write down any details about needed repair, replacement, or completion. Initial those items that you deem satisfactory. Keep one copy for your records, give the other copy to your remodeler.]

Item	Satis-factory	Needs Repair	Missing
Windows, doors, skylights	_____	_____	_____
Paint	_____	_____	_____
Flooring	_____	_____	_____
Drywall	_____	_____	_____
Cabinets and countertops	_____	_____	_____
Light fixtures	_____	_____	_____
Plumbing fixtures	_____	_____	_____
Heating, ventilation, and air-conditioning	_____	_____	_____
Appliances	_____	_____	_____
Accessories	_____	_____	_____
Smoke detectors	_____	_____	_____
Clean-up	_____	_____	_____
Landscaping	_____	_____	_____

Notes _____

_____

_____

_____

_____

more likely to get the desired result—a job completed to the specifications in your contract. During your examination, pay special attention to the items described in the following paragraphs.

Windows, Doors, and Skylights

Do windows, doors, and skylights open and close properly? Check to be sure that any hardware the painter removed before painting has been replaced. If you ordered skylight extension poles, have you received them? If your project calls for screens and/or snap-in grilles, be sure they are in place and that your remodeler gives you all keys to all your doors.

Paint

As careful as workers can be, certain areas inevitably will require touch-up paint. For example, baseboards often are nicked during carpet installation and final heating hook-ups. Even as the job winds down, walls and ceilings can be damaged by an errant board or piece of trim. Check to be sure the paint used to touch-up blemished areas matches the original color.

Flooring

Carpeting. Make sure all the seams are down and tight and that raw edges are rolled or tucked. If the pad has been laid correctly and the carpet stretched properly, no air pockets or bubbles should show on the carpet surface.

Tile. Inspect tiles for cracks and make sure all seams are grouted and/or caulked. Who is responsible for sealing the grout? Some grouts cannot be sealed immediately after installation.

Vinyl. Check that all the vinyl floor covering is lying flat, the seams are glued down, and the patterns match.

Hardwood floors. Inspect your hardwood floors before you replace any furniture. Are sanding marks visible? Look at the cuts around mantels and fireplaces and the places where the floor meets the baseboard. Check for gaps and be sure all nail holes are filled with wood putty.

Drywall or Plaster

Drywall should be seamless with no cracks. Nail pops that occur as the space dries can be repaired later with a little joint compound and touch-up paint.

Cabinets and Countertops

Make sure the cabinetmaker or trim carpenter has installed all hardware, adjusted doors so that they line up properly, set the backsplash tight to the countertop, filed laminate tops to eliminate sharp edges, clamped down stainless steel sinks properly, and caulked in porcelain drop-in sinks.

Light Fixtures

Check that all light fixtures work and that trim kits on recessed lights are installed straight. Ceiling mounts should rest flush with the ceiling. Make sure switch plates cover the cut-outs for the outlet boxes, that lights switch from the correct station, and that the correct fixture or appliance is activated.

Plumbing Fixtures

Test that faucets work (hot water on left, cold on right) and that they are seated properly. Check that all drains are connected and functioning.

Heating, Ventilation, and Air-Conditioning (HVAC)

Try all thermostats to make sure they operate the appropriate heat zone and that they turn in the correct direction. Check that all grates or grilles have been installed on forced-air systems. All trim pieces, such as end caps and corners, should be in place on a baseboard heating system.

Appliances

Be sure all appliances have been installed, leveled, and are in working condition. If your new refrigerator has an ice maker, be sure it is connected and dispenses ice.

Smoke Detectors

Smoke detectors are required by law in many jurisdictions. They must be installed according to code and be tested during the final inspection.

Accessories

Check installation of accessories such as mirrors, towel racks, pot racks, open shelves or rails for china and other collectibles, closet poles and shelves, and wire baskets.

Landscaping

Your landscaping plans may be as grand or as simple as your remodeling project itself. Whichever option you chose, thoroughly inspect the grounds to be sure all materials are properly planted and suitably placed.

Depending on the geographic location of your job and the time of year, your landscaping may be delayed a season or two to take advantage of the weather. If so, ask your remodeler to give you the new start and completion dates in writing.

Product Demonstrations

Ask your remodeler to demonstrate the new products in your home. For example, learn how windows tilt in for cleaning, how to make minor adjustments to doors, how to clean your gutters, and how to regulate your thermostats. I take notes or use a tape recorder to capture my remodeler's instructions, and I always try the operating and maintenance procedures myself with my remodeler present to offer advice. Expect your newly remodeled house to go through an adjustment period. Don't be disheartened if your house needs minor corrections. For example, if your home is built out of wood, remember that wood shrinks and moves. Therefore your drywall or plaster may crack in certain areas. A sliding glass door may require adjustment after a few weeks' use. Contact your remodeler before attempting any repairs yourself because any unauthorized tinkering could invalidate a manufacturer's warranty.

However regular maintenance of your home is your responsibility. The National Association of Home Builders recommends that you have these tools and supplies on hand for everyday use:

- medium-sized adjustable wrench
- standard pliers
- needle-nose pliers with wire cutter
- small, medium, and large screwdrivers with both standard and Phillips heads
- electric screwdriver
- claw hammer
- rubber mallet
- hand saw
- assorted nails, brads, screws, nuts, bolts, and washers
- level
- plane
- small electric drill
- caulking gun
- putty knife
- retractable measuring tape

Owner's Manuals and Warranty Cards

Ask your remodeler to turn over all product documents to you at the completion of the job. These documents may include owner's manuals, warranty cards, and use and care guides for all appliances, countertops, cabinets, and other major building parts. Ordinarily these documents are either affixed to the outside of the product's original storage box or placed inside the container, so be sure to ask your remodeler ahead of time to save all important product information. You could store these documents in a binder with pocket pages, a file box, or other container.

The manufacturers and subcontractors who made or installed the various parts and equipment in your house will be responsible for handling some of the service problems that arise while you are living in the house. However, you are responsible for the day-to-day maintenance of your new home.

—Your New Home and How to Take Care of It, *Home Builder Press, 1995*

Clean-Up

As anxious as you may be to have the last worker depart, resist the temptation to do the final cleaning yourself. Clean-up after a remodeling project should be left to the professionals because it often requires (a) industrial-strength cleaning products to remove sticky adhesives and dripped paint and (b) heavy-duty equipment to extract dust.

If your remodeler has consistently worked on dust containment, the final clean-up should go smoothly. But dust has a way of permeating every crevice during a project, so insist that all surfaces—even those out-of-reach places such as corner cabinets and soffits—are taken care of in the final cleaning. Depending on the nature of the project and the cleaning method used, airborne particles may continue to settle around your home for months. Special vacuum cleaners and bags can prevent recirculating the dust (see Sources).

Will the remodeler remove window stickers and other product decals? What about the exterior? Who is responsible for finding and removing nails in the driveway? You would be surprised how many loose nails can fall to the ground during a roofing or siding project. I picked up hundreds of stainless steel nails from my yard and driveway months after my roofer departed.

Final Details

Completion Certificates. Some jobs require only a final inspection, others require a certificate of occupancy. As discussed earlier in this chapter, a certificate of occupancy certifies that the structure is fit for habitation. Certificates of occupancy are granted only after your job's plumbing, electrical, and mechanical work pass inspection. Additionally, if you have installed, altered, repaired, or upgraded a septic system on your property, you must show a certificate of conformance for this work before you receive a certificate of occupancy.

Retainages. This money held back from final payment helps to protect you from problems that may arise during the first 30 days after your project's completion. If your contract contained a retainage clause, you usually have 30 days from the date of the certificate of occupancy to report any defective products or deficient work. If the remodeler has satisfied all obligations at the end of the 30 days, you must surrender the full retained amount (see Chapter 5).

Final Payment. Unless you wrote a retainage clause into your contract, your remodeler will expect the project's final payment when it is due according to your contract, for example, when you receive the certificate of occupancy or when the landscaping is finished. The criteria for receiving a certificate of occupancy don't necessarily correspond to the items on your punchlist. The building inspector is more concerned with health and safety issues than aesthetics. For example, you can receive a certificate of occupancy even if all your cabinet hardware is not installed, so you are technically responsible for making the final payment to your remodeler. If items are missing or some of the work is incomplete, you might want to retain a portion of the final payment until your remodeler corrects the deficiencies. If you decide to hold money back, you should negotiate a reasonable amount with your remodeler. Withholding other funds unfairly penalizes your remodeler. For example, if a specially ordered light fixture you chose is not going to arrive for another 8 weeks, you might withhold funds equal to the cost including installation.

House Warming Party

For many homeowners, completion of a remodeling project elicits a festive mood. A new kitchen, family room, or addition seems to inspire plans for a housewarming party. Often the bonding and camaraderie that develop among you, your remodeler, and the crew precipitate a mixture of emotions. While happy to regain your home, you may feel a sense of loss. Perhaps you would like to show your appreciation by throwing a party and inviting your remodeler, the crew, and the subcontractors to celebrate with you, your family, and friends. Or you might consider an open house for your family and friends and invite only your remodeler, so he or she can answer any technical questions your guests may ask. This project has been a team venture, and its completion provides a way to celebrate the victory together.

Chapter 9

Satisfaction Guaranteed: Understanding Warranties

In a perfect world a chapter about warranties would be unnecessary because nothing would ever go wrong. But in reality and in most remodeling projects, things do go wrong—faucets drip; doors, drawers, and windows sometimes stick; nails in drywall pop. Fine-tuning is a natural part of the remodeling process. If you accept the minor glitches that are bound to crop up, you'll be in a much better frame of mind to take care of them. The best way to resolve loose ends, product defects, and lapses in quality is to understand the warranties that govern the quality of work and materials in your newly remodeled space.

A warranty is a promise that the work and products that have gone into your project will meet certain standards. If either is inferior or defective, a warranty describes the actions that the remodeler and/or the manufacturer will take to remedy the defects.

Why Do You Need Warranty Protection?

Even the best remodeler cannot guarantee a defect-free project because the characteristics of the materials are as varied as the project itself. For example, lumber moves: it expands and contracts. Doors can warp and windows can develop stress cracks. If the polyurethane used to seal wood floors was improperly mixed in the factory, it can discolor through no fault of the installer.

Perhaps Dick Hallberg of Hallberg Remodeling Company in Portland, Oregon, explained this situation best: "Human beings make mistakes. Materials may fail. Homeowners should be more concerned with the manner and timeliness in which a remodeler deals with the inevitable problems that crop up during remodeling. The good news is, most of these problems will be minor and will occur within the first year after completion."

Terms, Conditions, and Limits of Coverage

The terms, conditions, and limits of coverage vary from remodeler to remodeler, state to state, and manufacturer to manufacturer. Use the worksheet in Figure 9-1 to help you understand the effect warranties can have on your project.

Express and Implied Warranties

An express warranty is a written or oral promise that obligates a remodeler to remedy any defects resulting from faulty materials or workmanship within a certain period of time.

Implied warranties are imposed by courts and legislatures, apart from any representations made by the remodeler. Two of the most common types of implied warranties are for habitability and good workmanship. According to David S. Jaffe, Staff Counsel for the National Association of

A warranty is a contract, and as such, it should clearly express the intent of the owner and the remodeler including (a) the scope of the warranty—what is covered and, just as importantly, what is not covered—and (b) the quality or performance standards that will determine whether an item is defective, and if so, how it will be corrected. For example, the warranty might provide that minor cracking in the foundation is not warranted, and the quality standards would define a minor crack.

—David S. Jaffe, Staff Counsel, National Association of Home Builders, Washington, D.C.

Home Builders, "The implied warranty of habitability means that a home must be structurally sound, must provide its inhabitants with a reasonably safe and sanitary place to live, and must be reasonably fit for human habitation. Under the implied warranty of good workmanship, the structure must be built to the standard of quality prevailing at the time and place of construction."

Extent of Coverage

Many remodelers limit coverage to the labor and materials needed to correct a problem, so secondary efforts may be your responsibility. For example, your remodeler may repair a squeaky floor, but he or she may not replace the furniture and rugs. Who will paint your wall or ceiling after the nail pops in drywall are replaced?

Who is liable for consequential damage, secondary damage that occurs because of defective workmanship or materials? For example, suppose that during a second-floor remodeling project, a leaking roof damages your furniture, rugs, and other personal belongings. If the remodeler or a subcontractor was negligent, then the contractor's liability insurance should cover the loss. On the other hand, if months or years after completion of the project, your roof sustains damage in a storm or fire, then your homeowner's insurance should pay for the damage.

Figure 9-1. Warranty Terms, Conditions, and Limits of Coverage

[Prepare these forms in advance and save time later should a claim situation arise. You can use this worksheet to record the terms, conditions, and limits of your remodeler's and manufacturers' warranties. Duplicate the manufacturer's part of this form for each of your warranties, or copy the information onto index cards for your records.]

Remodeler's Warranty

Name _____

Street address _____

City, state, zip _____

Phone (_____) _____ Duration of coverage _____

Quality standards used (name of publication or language used guiding the remodeler's standards of workmanship and materials) _____

_____

State law mandates _____

Manufacturer's Warranty Information

Manufacturer's name _____

Product _____

Street address _____

City, state, zip _____

Phone (_____) _____ Contact person _____

Duration of warranty _____ Type of warranty _____

Warranty covers _____

_____ Parts, labor, or both _____

Where serviced _____

Date owner's manuals and warranty cards received _____

Date product registration card mailed _____

Care instructions _____

_____

Who Backs Your Warranty?

Your home is made up of a variety of systems. The wood or steel frame forms the structure; windows and doors provide ventilation and a place to enter and exit; pipes, ducts, and fixtures generate heat; and so on. Your remodeler and subcontractors are responsible for installing those systems in a professional manner, but what about the parts of each system—the framing lumber, the windows and doors themselves, the furnace or boiler? Each major part has its own manufacturer- or dealer-backed warranty (Figure 9-2). Determine which manufacturers' warranties extend to you; some guarantees pass only to the remodeler.

Use the worksheet in Figure 9-1 to keep track of the names and addresses of all parties providing warranty coverage on your project. File this information so it is easily accessible later.

Remodeler's Warranty

As trustworthy and reputable as your remodeler may be, a handshake and a promise are not enough. For peace of mind, be sure your remodeler puts his or her intentions in writing. Knowing where you stand at the beginning of your project can prevent costly misunderstandings and legal action later.

Like the remodeling contract itself, the warranty agreement between you and your remodeler should be explicit, intelligible, and fair to both parties (Figures 9-3 and 9-4).

How long will your remodeler warrant defects in the quality of the work and materials? Some remodelers offer protection for a few months or for 1, 2, or 5 years. However, some states have strict consumer protection laws that may hold him or her responsible for major structural defects for 10 years or more. If in doubt, contact your state building commissioner. Some remodelers, bound more by duty than a date, will respond to your needs long after the express warranty has expired.

Your idea of a defect in workmanship and materials and your remodeler's idea may differ. Your remodeler should provide standards against which to judge whether he or she is complying with the warranty. According to *Contracts and Liability for Builders and Remodelers*, 3rd ed., "In the absence of such standards the remodeler and the homeowner may find themselves

Photo courtesy of Defern Contracting, Inc., Brookfield, New Hampshire

Figure 9-2. Remodeler Giving Owner's Manuals and Warranties to Client

Notify your remodeler in advance that you want to collect all owner's manuals and warranty cards so that you will have them handy if you need them. Obtain owner's manuals and warranty cards during construction.

Figure 9-3. Sample of Remodeler's Limited Warranty Agreement

(Excluding Items Covered by the Magnuson-Moss Act)

This limited warranty agreement is extended by ___(remodeler's name)___, (the remodeler), whose address is ___(remodeler's address)___, to ___(owner's name)___, (the owner) of the property at the following address:[1]

_____

_____

_____

_____

> **This limited warranty excludes consequential damages, limits the duration of implied warranties, and provides for liquidated damages.**

1. What Is Covered by the Warranty?

The remodeler warrants that all construction related to the _[remodeling, renovation, rehabilitation, restoration, or addition]_ substantially conforms with the plans and specifications and change orders for this job. The remodeler warrants that during the first thirty (30) days after the owner occupies the remodeled space, the remodeler will adjust or correct minor defects, omissions, or malfunctions, such as missing equipment or hardware; sticking doors, drawers, and windows; dripping faucets; and other minor malfunctions reported by the owner upon inspection of the _[remodeled, renovated, rehabilitated, restored, or added]_ space.

Within one (1) year from the date of substantial completion or use of the _[remodeled, renovated, rehabilitated, restored, or added]_ space by the owner, whichever is first, the remodeler will repair or replace, at the remodeler's option, any latent defects in material or workmanship by the standards of construction relevant in _(city, state)_. A *latent defect* is defined as one which was not apparent or ascertainable at the time of occupancy. The owner agrees to accept a reasonable match in any repair or replacement in the event the original item is no longer available.

2. What Is Not Covered

This limited warranty does not cover the following items:

A. Damage resulting from fires, floods, storms, electrical malfunctions, accidents, nor acts of God
B. Damage from alterations, misuse, or abuse of the covered items by any person

C. Damage resulting from the owner's failure to observe any operating instructions furnished by the remodeler at the time of installation
D. Damage resulting from a malfunction of equipment or lines of the telephone, gas, power, or water companies
E. Any items listed as nonwarrantable conditions on the list that is incorporated into this contract (The owner acknowledges receipt of the list of nonwarrantable conditions.) _____
(owner's initials)
F. Any item furnished or installed by the owner
G. Any appliance, piece of equipment, or other item that is a consumer product for the purposes of the Magnuson-Moss Warranty Act, 15 U.S.C. Sec. 2301 et seq., installed or included in the owner's property

The only warranties of items listed below are those that the manufacturer provides to the owner:[2]

Appliances

Clothes dryer	Ice maker	Oven and hood
Clothes washer	Kitchen center	Refrigerator
Dishwasher	(a type of	Range, stove,
Freezer	food proces-	or cooktop
Garbage	sor)	Trash com-
disposal	Microwave	pactor

Heating and Ventilation

Air-conditioning	Exhaust fan	Space heater
Boiler	Furnace	Thermostat
Electronic air	Heat pump	
cleaner	Humidifier	

Mechanical and/or Electrical

Burglar alarm	Garage door	Water meter
Central vacuum	opener	Water pump
system	Gas meter	
Chimes	Gas or electric	
Electric meter	barbecue grill	
Fire alarm	Intercom	
Fire extinguisher	Smoke detector	

Plumbing

Garbage	Sump pump	Water softener
disposal	Water heater	Whirlpool bath[3]

---

1. This form is designed for a single owner. If more than one owner is involved, it should be adapted to accommodate the initials and signature of each of the owners.
2. Remodelers should exclude from this list any items that are not applicable to the job for which the warranty is being provided. For instance, if the job did not involve any kitchen appliances, the remodeler need not include them in the list.]
3. **Warning**—This list is not exclusive.

Source: Reprinted from *Contracts and Liability for Builders and Remodelers*, 3rd ed. (Washington, D.C.: Home Builder Press, 1993).

Figure 9-3. Sample of Remodeler's Limited Warranty Agreement (Continued)

The following items are not consumer products under the Magnuson-Moss Warranty Act when sold as part of a new home:

Heating and Ventilation

Duct	Radiator	Register

Mechanical and/or Electrical

Circuit breaker	Electric panel	Garage door
Electrical switch	box	Light fixture
and outlet	Fuse	Wiring

Plumbing

Bidet	head, faucet,	Sink
Bathtub	trap, escutch-	Shower stall
Medicine	eon [flange	Sprinkler head
cabinet	around a pipe	Toilet
Plumbing fit-	or fitting], and	Vanity
tings (shower	drain)	

Miscellaneous Items

Cabinet	Floor covering	Shelving
Ceiling	(includes	Shingles
Chimney and	carpeting,	Wall or wall
fireplace	linoleum, tile,	covering
Door	parquet)	Window
Fencing	Gutter	

The following separate items of equipment are not consumer products under the magnuson-Moss Act when sold as part of a condominium, cooperative, or similar multiple-family dwelling . . . [because] they are not normally used for "personal, family, or household purposes" within the meaning of the Act:

Elevator
Emergency back-up generator
Institutional trash compactor
Fusible fire door closer
Master TV antenna
TV security monitor

(1) The remodeler has made any such warranties available to the owner for the owner's inspection and the owner acknowledges receipt of copies of any warranties requested.

_____
(owner's initials)

(2) The remodeler hereby assigns (to the extent that they are assignable) and conveys to the owner all warranties provided to the remodeler on any manufactured items that have been installed or included in the owner's property. The owner accepts this assignment and acknowledges that the remodeler's only

responsibility relating to such items is to lend assistance to the owner in settling any claim resulting from the installation of these products. _____ _____
(owner's initials)   (remodeler's initials)

3. Remedies and Limitations

A. The owner understands that the sole remedies under this limited warranty agreement are repair and replacement as set forth here.

_____
(owner's initials)

B. With respect to any claim whatsoever asserted by the owner against the remodeler, the owner understands that the owner will have no right to recover or request compensation for, and the remodeler shall not be liable for, any of the following items:

(1) Incidental, consequential, secondary, or punitive damages

(2) Damages for aggravation, mental anguish, emotional distress, or pain and suffering

(3) Attorney's fees or costs _____
(owner's initials)

C. The remodeler hereby limits the duration of all implied warranties, including the warranties of workmanship and materials to one (1) year from the date of sale or the date of substantial completion, whichever comes first. _____
(owner's initials)

D. These limitations shall be enforceable to the extent permitted by law. Some states do not allow the exclusion or limitation of incidental or consequential damages or the limitation of implied warranties, so the limitations or exclusions listed above may not apply.

[Alternative to 3C

[C. The owner understands that no implied warranties whatsoever apply to the structure of the __[remodeling, renovation, rehabilitation, or restoration of or addition to]__ the house and items that are functionally part of the __[remodeling, renovation, rehabilitation, or restoration of or addition to]__ the house. The remodeler disclaims any implied warranties, including (but not limited to) warranties of workmanship and materials to the extent allowed by law, and any implied warranty that exists despite this disclaimer is limited to a period of one (1) year. These limitations shall be enforceable to the extent permitted by the law. Some states do not allow limitations on how long an implied warranty lasts, so this limitation may not apply._____
(owner's initials)

Figure 9-3. Sample of Remodeler's Limited Warranty Agreement (Continued)

[The owner acknowledges acceptance of these limitations on the warranties offered by the remodeler in consideration for this limited warranty and the other provisions of the construction contract. Therefore, the owner agrees to these limitations if, notwithstanding the provisions of the limited warranty, liability should arise on the part of the remodeler.]

D. Notwithstanding the provisions of this limited warranty agreement, if any liability arises on the part of the remodeler, the remodeler will pay the amount of actual provable damages arising from such liability, but the amount shall not exceed $_____. This amount, fixed as liquidated damages and not as a penalty, shall be the remodeler's complete and exclusive amount of liability. The provisions of this paragraph apply if loss or damage results directly or indirectly to persons or property from the performance or failure to perform obligations imposed by the construction contract or from negligence, active or otherwise, of the remodeler, the remodeler's agents, or employees.

The owner (a) understands that this provision limits the damages for which the remodeler will be liable and (b) acknowledges acceptance of this liquidated damages provision in consideration for the limited warranties provided by the remodeler and the other provisions of the construction contract. Therefore, the owner agrees to this liquidated damages clause if, notwithstanding the provisions of this limited warranty, liability should arise on the part of the remodeler. _____
<u>(owner's initials)</u>

E. This warranty is personal to the original owner of the _[remodeling, renovation, rehabilitation, or restoration of or addition to]_ the house and does not run with the property, the _[remodeling, renovation, or rehabilitation of or addition to]_ the house nor with the items contained in the house. The original owner may not assign, transfer, or convey this warranty without the prior written consent of the remodeler.

4. How to Obtain Service

If a problem develops during the warranty period, the owner should notify the remodeler in writing at the address given above of the specific problem. The written statement of the problem should include the owner's name, address, telephone number, and a description of the nature of the problem. The remodeler will begin performing the obligations under this warranty within a reasonable time of the remodeler's receipt of such a request and will diligently pursue these obligations.

Repair work will be done during the remodeler's normal working hours except where delay will cause additional damage. The owner agrees to provide the remodeler or remodeler's representative access to the house and the presence during the work of a responsible adult with the authority to approve the repair and sign a call-back ticket upon completion of the repair.

5. Specific Legal Rights

This limited warranty gives the owner specific legal rights, and the owner may also have other rights which vary from state to state.

6. Where to Get Help

If the owner wants help or information concerning this warranty, the owner should contact the remodeler.

7. The Only Warranty Give by the Remodeler

The owner acknowledges (a) that the owner has thoroughly examined the _[remodeling, renovation, rehabilitation, or restoration of or addition to]_ the house that is to be conveyed, (b) the buyer has read and understands the limited warranty, and (c) that the remodeler has made no guarantees, warranties, understandings, nor representations (nor have any been made by any representatives of the remodeler) that are not set forth in this document.

I acknowledge having read, understood, and received a copy of this limited warranty agreement.

_____   _____
        (owner)   (remodeler)

Date _____   By_____

                         Title _____

                         Date _____

Figure 9-4. Sample Statement of Nonwarrantable Conditions

This statement of conditions that are not subject to the ___[builder's or remodeler's]___ warranties explains some of the changes and need for maintenance that may occur in a ___[new house or a house that is remodeled, renovated, rehabilitated, or restored or added to]___ over the first year or so of occupancy. A house requires more maintenance and care than most products because it is made of many different components, each with its own special characteristics.

The ___[buyer or owner]___ [1] understands that like other products made by humans, a ___[a house or a house that is remodeled, renovated, rehabilitated, restored, or added to]___ is not perfect. It will show some minor flaws and unforeseeable defects, and it may require some adjustments and touching up.

As described in the limited warranty provided to the ___[buyer or owner]___ of which this statement of Nonwarrantable Conditions is made a part, the ___[builder or remodeler]___ will correct certain defects that arise during defined time periods after construction is completed. Other items that are not covered by the ___[builder's or remodeler's]___ warranty may be covered by manufacturers' warranties.

Some conditions, including (but not limited to) those listed in this statement of nonwarrantable conditions, are not covered under the ___[builder's or remodeler's]___ warranties. The ___[buyer or owner]___ should read these carefully and understand that the ___[buyer or owner]___ has not contracted for the ___[builder or remodeler]___ to correct certain types of problems that may occur in ___[the buyer's house or the owner's remodeled, renovated, rehabilitated, restored, or added space]___. These guidelines will alert the ___[buyer or owner]___ to certain types of maintenance (a) that are the responsibility of the ___[buyer or owner]___ and (b) that could lead to problems if they are neglected.

The following list outlines some of the conditions that are not warranted by the ___[builder or remodeler]___. The ___[buyer or owner]___ should be sure to understand this list. If the ___[buyer or owner]___ has any questions, ___[he or she]___ should ask the ___[builder or remodeler]___ and feel free to consult an attorney before signing the acknowledgment.

[Of the items listed and discussed below, remodelers might want to include only those that pertain to a particular job in the warranty for that job because many of the items would not apply to every job.]

1. Concrete

Concrete foundations, steps, walks, drives, and patios can develop cracks that do not affect the structural integrity of the building. These cracks are caused by characteristics of the concrete itself. No reasonable method of eliminating these cracks exists. This condition does not affect the strength of the building.

2. Masonry and Mortar

Masonry and mortar can develop cracks from shrinkage of either the mortar or the brick. This condition is normal and should not be considered a defect.

3. Wood

Wood will sometimes check or crack or the fibers will spread apart because of the drying out process. This condition is most often caused by the heat inside the house or the exposure to the sun on the outside of the house. This condition is considered normal, and the homeowner is responsible for any maintenance or repairs resulting from it.

4. Sheetrock and Drywall

Sheetrock or drywall will sometimes develop nail pops or settlement cracks. These nail pops and settlement cracks are a normal part of the drying out process. These items can easily be handled by the homeowner with spackling during normal redecorating. However, if the homeowner wishes, the ___[builder or remodeler]___ will send a worker at the end of one (1) year to make the necessary repairs. The ___[builder's or remodeler's]___ repairs will not include repainting.

5. Floor Squeaks

After extensive research and writing on the subject, technical experts have concluded that much has been tried but that little can be done about floor squeaks. Generally, floor squeaks will appear and disappear over time with changes in the weather and other phenomenon.

6. Floors

Floors are not warranted for damage caused by neglect or the incidents of use. Wood, tile, and carpet all require maintenance. Floor casters are recommended to prevent scratching or chipping of wood or tile, and stains should be cleaned from carpets, wood, or tile immediately to prevent discoloration. Carpet has a tendency to loosen in damp weather and will stretch tight again in dryer weather.

---

1. This form is designed for a single buyer or owner. If more than one buyer or owner is involved, the form should be adapted to accommodate the initials and signature of each of the buyers or owners.

Source: Reprinted from *Contracts and Liability for Builders and Remodelers*, 3rd ed. (Washington, D.C.: Home Builder Press, 1993).

Figure 9-4. Sample Statement of Nonwarrantable Conditions (continued)

7. Caulking

Exterior caulking and interior caulking in bathtubs, shower stalls, and ceramic tile surfaces will crack or bleed somewhat in the months after installation. These conditions are normal and should not be considered a problem. Any maintenance or repairs resulting from them are the homeowner's responsibility.

8. Bricks Discoloration

Most bricks may discolor because of the elements, rain run-off, weathering, or bleaching. Efflorescence—the formation of salts on the surface of brick walls—may occur because of the passage of moisture through the wall. Efflorescence is a common occurrence, and the home owner can clean these areas as the phenomenon occurs.

9. Broken Glass

Any broken glass or mirrors that are not noted by the __[buyer or owner]__ on the final inspection form are the responsibility of the __[buyer or owner]__ .

10. Frozen Pipes

The __[buyer or owner]__ must take precautions to prevent freezing of pipes and sillcocks during cold weather, such as removing outside hoses from sillcocks, leaving faucets with a slight drip, and turning off the water system if the house is to be left for extended periods during cold weather.

11. Stained Wood

All items that are stained will normally have a variation of colors because of the different textures of the woods. Because of weather changes, doors that have panels will sometimes dry out and leave a small space of bare wood, which the home owner can easily touch up. These normal conditions should not be considered defects.

12. Paint

Good quality paint has been used internally and externally on this home. Nevertheless, exterior paint can sometimes crack or check. The source of this defect is most often something other than the paint. To avoid problems with the paint, __[buyer or owner]__ should avoid allowing lawn sprinklers to hit painted areas, washing down painted areas, and so on. __[buyer or owner]__ should also not scrub latex-painted, inside walls and be careful of newly painted walls as they move furniture. The best paint will be stained or chipped if it is not cared for properly. Any defects in painting that are not noted at final inspection are the __[buyer's or owner's]__ responsibility.

13. Cosmetic Items

The __[buyer or owner]__ has not contracted with the __[builder or remodeler]__ to cover ordinary wear and tear or other occurrences subsequent to construction that affect the condition of features in the home. Chips, scratches, or mars in tile, woodwork, walls, porcelain, brick, mirrors, plumbing fixtures, marble and formica tops, lighting fixtures, kitchen and other appliances, doors, paneling, siding, screens, windows, carpet, vinyl floors, cabinets, and the like that are not recognized and noted by the __[buyer or owner]__ at the final inspection are nonwarrantable conditions, and the upkeep of any cosmetic aspect of the __[house or the remodeled, renovated, rehabilitated, restored, or added space]__ is the __[buyer's or owner's]__ responsibility.

14. Plumbing

Dripping faucets, toilet adjustments, and toilet seats are covered by the __[builder's or remodeler's]__ warranty for a _____-day (____) period only. After that, they are the __[buyer's or owner's]__ responsibility. If the plumbing is stopped up during the warranty period and the person servicing the plumbing finds foreign materials in the line, the __[buyer or owner]__ will be billed for the call.

15. Alterations to Grading

The __[buyer's or owner's]__ lot has been graded to ensure proper drainage away from __[the home or the remodeled, renovated, rehabilitated, restored, or added space]__ . Should the __[buyer or owner]__ want to change the drainage pattern because of landscaping, installation of patio or service walks, or other reasons, the __[buyer or owner]__ should be sure to retain a proper drainage slope. The __[builder or remodeler]__ assumes no responsibility for the grading or subsequent flooding or stagnant pool formation if the established pattern is altered.

16. Lawn and Shrubs

The __[builder or remodeler]__ accepts no responsibility for the growth of grass or shrubs. Once the __[builder or remodeler]__ grades, seeds and/or sods, and fertilizes the yard, the __[buyer or owner]__ must water the plants and grass the proper amount and plant ground cover, where necessary to prevent erosion. The builder will not regrade a yard, nor remove or replace any shrubs or trees, except for those that are noted as diseased at final inspection.

Figure 9-4. Sample Statement of Nonwarrantable Conditions (continued)

17. Roof

During the first year the warranty on the ___[buyer's roof or the roof of an owner's addition]___ is for workmanship and materials. After that the warranty on the roof is for material only, and it is prorated over the period of the lifetime use of the roof. Warranty claims for any defects in materials will be handled with the manufacturer with the ___[builder's or remodeler's]___ assistance. The ___[builder or remodeler]___ will not be responsible for any damages caused by walking on the roof or by installing a television antenna or other item on the roof.

18. Heating and Air-Conditioning

The ___[buyer's or owner's]___ source of heating and air-conditioning is covered by a manufacturer's warranty. The buyer is responsible for making sure the filters are kept clean and changed on a 30-day basis. Failure to do so may void the warranty. Having the equipment serviced or checked at least yearly is a good idea.

19. Indoor Air Quality

[An appropriate disclaimer and warning regarding possible indoor air quality problems, including radon, should be inserted here by the ___[builder or remodeler]___. (See Chapter 5.)]

I acknowledge having read and understood and received a copy of the above outline of nonwarrantable items. I understand and agree that these are conditions for which we have not contracted and will not hold the builder liable.

_____   _____
(buyer or owner)   (builder or remodeler)

Date _____   By _____

Title _____.

Date _____

---

at odds if the owner's personal standards differ from industry standards. If the parties do not spell out the construction standards, they run the risk of having a court decide for them." For more information about industry standards, ask to borrow your remodeler's copy of the Home Builder Press publication, *Quality Standards for the Professional Remodeler*, 2nd ed., or contact the publisher directly (see Selected Bibliography).

Manufacturer's Warranty

The manufacturers of the products in your project may provide additional warranties. (As discussed in Chapter 8, your remodeler already should have given you all owner's manuals and warranty cards.) For example, Andersen Windows offers a 20-year warranty on glass and 1-year warranty on all components, including hardware.

Always report a product defect to your remodeler first. Your remodeler is your first line of defense when dealing with a manufacturer. Manufacturers usually will replace a defective piece. For example, in the case of a defective window, the manufacturer may provide you with a new piece of glass, but you or your remodeler may have to pay for the installation and/or finishing.

Insurance-Backed Warranty

Some remodelers offer extended warranty coverage through an insurance-backed program. At this time, only Residential Warranty Corporation (RWC) warrants remodeling work (see Sources). Coverage includes a 1-year warranty against faulty work and materials, a 2-year warranty against defects in major systems, such as plumbing and wiring, and additional structural coverage lasting for 3 to 5 years.

With an insurance-backed warranty, a private insurance company will step in to honor the warranty if your remodeler goes out of business or will not take care of the problem. Such a warranty can be a powerful marketing tool, but don't let its presence, alone, sway you. In other words, if you suspect a contractor may not be around to honor your warranty, why would you do business with that individual in the first place? An insurance-backed warranty shouldn't lull you into a false sense of security.

While quality is a relative term, and standards of quality vary, we subscribe to and exceed the quality standards developed and set forth by the Remodelors® Council of the National Association of Home Builders in the manual titled **Quality Standards for the Professional Remodeler***, 2nd ed.*

—Bill Gaver, President, Defern Contracting, Inc., Brookfield, New Hampshire

The Callback and the Request for Service

Professional remodelers take warranty work seriously. Diligent remodelers usually contact homeowners before the 6-month or 1-year anniversary of a project's completion to inquire about items in need of repair or adjustment. A reputable remodeler doesn't dread these calls but sees them as opportunities to reconnect with a valued customer, to learn ways to improve procedures, and perhaps to provide additional services.

Instead of calling my remodeler every time something needs adjustment, I keep an ongoing punchlist of minor defects, such as a cracked tile or a missing screen. I present this entire list at a prearranged time within the warranty period. Of course, if something major happens—your heating system fails or your roof leaks—contact your remodeler at once.

Additional Work or Home Maintenance

Once you're enjoying your new space, memories of those weeks and months you spent planning and rebuilding your home will begin to fade. Then one day, when you least expect it, you may begin thinking of yet another project. My sunroom was born when I found myself thinking after a stressful day, "Wouldn't a spa or hot tub be great right about now?" Or maybe you'll be relaxing outdoors after dinner when you decide you'd like a screened-in porch. That desire to improve your surroundings has come back, but now you know what to expect. This time you have the knowledge and the wisdom gained from the previous project to guide you.

Because I'm on a limited budget with several large projects yet to do, I've planned my home improvements and remodeling work in phases. If you're considering more work on your property, a call-back is an excellent time to start planning with your remodeler.

Staying in Touch with Your Remodeler

Most remodelers want to develop long-term relationships with their clients. Your remodeler probably hopes this project will be the first of many you will do together and that you'll recommend the firm for other jobs. I think of my remodeler as an ally in the ever-changing, complex world of homeownership, a valuable team member who offers time, talent, and tools to ensure that my home keeps up with my needs. Next year you might decide to add a deck or remodel a bathroom. Maybe you'll want the name of a reputable swimming pool contractor or landscape architect. Your remodeler is available to recommend such firms, answer questions, and help you turn your home improvement dreams into reality. In much the same way you call upon other trusted professionals—your doctor, your mechanic, your grocer—rely on your remodeler for expert home improvement advice.

Glossary

activity curve—The correlation between a homeowner's level of anxiety and the various stages of a remodeling project.

allowance—A specific dollar amount allocated by a remodeler for specified items in a contract for which brand, model number, color, size, or other detail is not yet known.

certificate of occupancy—A document from a local government department or agency to certify that a home or structure has met all code requirements and is fit for habitation or use.

change order—A legally binding, written document between a remodeler and a homeowner modifying methods, work, materials, or other aspect of the original contract, usually for a physical change in the work.

cost-plus contract—A contract between a remodeler and a homeowner based on the accrued cost of labor and materials plus a percentage for profit and overhead. Also known as a time-and-materials contract.

critical path—The sequence of events that dictates the scheduling of a remodeling project.

cross section—A drawing showing a cut-away portion of a detail.

dado—A slot cut into a piece of wood that another piece of wood fits into. Dados are commonly used in the construction of fixed bookshelves and door frames.

design-build firm—A remodeling or building firm engaged in both designing and building remodeling projects, houses, or other structures.

drywall—The paper-covered gypsum board that is fastened to the framing to create the interior walls and ceilings of a room or space.

elevations—Drawings showing the front, rear, and side exterior views of a structure.

encroachment—The accidental or deliberate building of a structure or a portion of a structure on someone else's property.

fixed-price contract—A contract between a remodeler and a homeowner based on a set price.

flashing—The metal or plastic material used to make a watertight seal between vertical and horizontal members on the outside of a home (such as a roof running into a sidewall) or for protection over a window or door.

footing—The base on which a foundation, deck, or stairs are built to support the weight, anchor the house, and help prevent settling.

footprint—The outermost dimensions or perimeter of a structure.

framing—The components of the structure of a building such as the joists and the studs. Framing also is the process of constructing the structure of a room or building.

grading—Moving soil to prepare a building site for construction; also, finish grading is the leveling and sloping of the soil around a building to direct groundwater away from it.

hidden conditions—Items or situations affecting a remodeling project that are not readily visible, such as disconnected pipes for a sink that was replaced and moved to a new location.

joists—The framing members of floors, ceilings, and roofs.

lien release—A document signed by subcontractors and vendors stating that they have been paid for the work they did or materials they supplied for a project.

progress payments—Payments a homeowner makes to a remodeler at predetermined intervals, such as when the rough-in work begins or when the roof is started.

punchlist—A list of missing items, unfinished tasks, and/or items needing correction that is developed and completed at the end of a remodeling project and periodically during the warranty period.

radon—A colorless, odorous gas that can leak up through the soil, penetrating a home and posing health concerns.

remodeling fever—A term used to describe the anxiety experienced by homeowners during the course of a remodeling project.

retainage—The practice of withholding a percentage of the contract price for an agreed-upon period to help ensure that the remodeler will correct defective materials and/or poor-quality work and supply missing (back-ordered) items.

setback requirement—The legally required distance between a structure and its property boundaries.

sheathing—The material placed on the exterior surfaces of a structure to allow for the installation of finished siding and roofing.

shim—A thin, often tapered piece of material used for leveling or filling space.

specifications—A detailed list or description of the known products, materials, quantities, and finishes to be used in the construction of a project.

subcontractor—An individual or firm that contracts with a remodeler to perform specific services such as plumbing, heating, and wiring.

variance—An exception to a zoning ordinance granted to a homeowner under special conditions.

workers' compensation insurance—Insurance carried by remodelers to protect employees in the event of a work-related accident.

working drawings—Drawings with enough detail for the contractor to actually build the project.

Sources

Listed below you will find suppliers of some of the items mentioned in this book. Inclusion in this list is not a recommendation for purchase by the author, Home Builder Press, nor the National Association of Home Builders. Some items may require a fee and may be available from other suppliers.

American Lighting Association (ALA), 2050 Stemmons Freeway, P.O. Box 580168, Dallas, TX 75342. (800) 605-4448. For *Lighting Your Life*.

CSC-Equifax, P.O. Box 740241, Atlanta, GA 30374. For credit check.

Environmental Protection Agency, Office of Radiation and Indoor Air, 401 M Street, SW, Mail Code RD6604J, Washington, DC 20460. (202) 233-9370. For *A Citizen's Guide to Radon: What It Is and What to Do About It*.

Fannie Mae HomeStyle Initiative. For details and a list of participating lenders, call (800) 732-6643 or Janice Mitchell at (202) 752-7953.

Home Builder Bookstore, National Association of Home Builders, 1201 15th St., NW, Washington, DC 20005-2800. (800) 223-2665 or fax (202) 822-0512. For catalog of Home Builder Press publications.

National Allergy Supply, P.O. Box 1658, 4400 Abbott's Bridge Road, Duluth, GA 30136. (800) 522-1448. For dustproof vacuum cleaner bags.

National Association of Home Builders (NAHB), 1201 15th Street, NW, Washington, DC 20005-2800. (202) 822-0200.

National Association of the Remodeling Industry (NARI), 4301 North Fairfax Drive, Suite 310, Arlington, VA 22203. (800) 966-7601.

National Kitchen and Bath Association (NKBA), 687 Willow Grove Street, Hackettstown, NJ 07840. (908) 852-0033 and (800) 367-6522. To verify membership call (800) 401-NKBA or write to P.O. Box 2375, Chatsworth, CA 91313.

Remodelors® Council, National Association of Home Builders (NAHB-RC), 1201 15th Street, NW, Washington, DC 20005. (202) 822-0216. For a free copy of the brochure, *How to Choose a Remodeler Who's on the Level*, send a business-size, number 10, self-addressed, stamped envelope.

Residential Warranty Corporation (RWC), 5300 Derry Street, Harrisburg, PA 17111-3598. (717) 561-4480 or (800) 247-1812.

Tile Promotion Board, Suite 211, 900 East Indiantown Road, Juniper, FL 33477. (800) 881-8453. For *Decorating with Ceramic Title*.

Trans Union Corporation, P.O. Box 2968, Witchita, KS 67201. For credit check.

TRW Complimentary Report Request, P.O. Box 2350, Chatsworth, CA 91313-2350. For credit check.

U.S. Department of Housing and Urban Development, 1726 18th Street, NW, Washington, DC 20009. (800) 733-4663. For information on HUD Title I Insurance Program.

VMP Mortgage Forms, 18050 15 Mile Road, Fraser, MI 48026. For *Rehab a Home with HUD's 203(K)*. HUD Publication Number 1220-H(1).

Selected Bibliography

Books and Pamphlets

Axelrod, Jerold L. *Architectural Plans for Adding On or Remodeling*. New York: TAB Books, 1992.

Baths and Kitchens. Newton, Conn.: Taunton Press, 1993.

Citizen's Guide to Radon: What It Is and What to Do About It, A. Washington, D.C.: The Environmental Protection Agency, 1992.

Contracts and Liability for Builders and Remodelers, 3rd ed. Washington, D.C.: Home Builder Press, National Association of Home Builders, 1993.

Decorating with Ceramic Tile. Juniper, Fla.: Tile Promotion Board, 1993.

Fireplace Designs. Crozet, Va.: Betterway Books, 1993.

Gilliatt, Mary. *The Decorating Book*. New York: Pantheon Books, 1995.

Gray, Johnny. *The Art of Kitchen Design*. New York: Sterling Publishing, 1994.

Greene, Fayal. *Anatomy of a House: A Picture Dictionary of Architectural and Design Elements*. New York: Doubleday, 1991.

Hilliard, Elizabeth. *Designing with Tiles*. New York: Abbeville Press, 1993.

How to Choose a Remodeler Who's on the Level. Washington, D.C.: Home Builder Press, National Association of Home Builders, 1991.

How to Choose a Remodeler Who's on the Level (video). Washington, D.C.: Home Builder Press, National Association of Home Builders, 1994.

Kilpatrick, John A. *Understanding House Construction*, 2nd ed. Washington, D.C.: Home Builder Press, National Association of Home Builders, 1993.

Kitchen and Source Book. New York: Sweets/McGraw-Hill, 1994.

Kitchen Planning Guidelines. Hackettstown, N.J.: National Kitchen and Bath Association, 1995.

Lighting Your Life. Dallas, Tex.: American Lighting Association, 1992.

Locke, Jim. *The Well-Built House: Everything You Need To Know Before Building a New House or Remodeling an Old One*. Boston: Houghton Mifflin Co., 1992.

Madden, Chris Casson. *Kitchens*. New York: Clarkson Potter, 1993.

McCloud, Kevin. *Lighting Style: The Complete Guide to Lighting Every Room in Your Home*. New York: Simon and Schuster, 1995.

Millard, Scott. *Deck Planner*. Tucson, Ariz.: Home Planners, Inc., 1990.

Munro, Candace Ord. *Family Room*. For Your Home Series. New York: Little, Brown and Co., 1994.

NAHB Remodelors® Council and National Research Center. *Quality Standards for the Professional Remodeler*. 2nd ed. Washington, D.C.: NAHB Home Builder Press, National Association of Home Builders, 1991.

Neibauer, Alan. *Home Improvement: Total Planning on Your Computer*. Emoryville, Calif.: Ziff-Davis Press, 1995 (with CD-ROM disk).

Painting and Wallpapering. San Ramone, Calif.: Ortho Books, Monsanto Co., 1984.

Phillip, Steven J. *Old House Dictionary: An Illustrated Guide to American Domestic Architecture (1600-1940)*. Washington, D.C.: Preservation Press, 1994.

Planning Kit, The. Hackettstown, N.J.: National Kitchen and Bath Association, 1995.

Rees, Yvonne, and Tony Herbert. *Floor Style: A Sourcebook of Ideas for Transforming the World Beneath Your Feet*. New York: Nostrand Reinhold, 1989.

Rehab a Home with HUD's 203(K). HUD Publication Number 1220-H(1). Fraser, Mich.: VMP Mortgage Forms, 1994.

Thomas, Steve, and Philip Langdon. *This Old House Bathrooms: A Guide to Design and Renovation*. New York: Little, Brown and Co., 1993.

Yepsen, Roger. *Adding On*. Emmaus, Pa.: Rodale Press, Inc., 1995.

Your New Home and How to Take Care of It. Washington, D.C.: Home Builder Press, National Association of Home Builders, 1995.

Articles

Benderoff, Eric. "Inside Remodeling Today." *Remodeled Homes*, No. 4, 1994.

Holmes, Kendall. "1994-95 Cost Vs. Value Report." *Remodeling*, November 1994. (Published annually.) Available from *Remodeling* Reprints, One Thomas Circle, NW, Suite 600, Washington, DC 20005. (202) 452-0800.

_____. "Stop Thieves." *Remodeling*, March 1994.

Lowe, Linda. "Annual Buyer's Guide." *Builder,* April 1994. (Published annually.) One Thomas Circle, NW, Suite 600, Washington, DC 20005. (202) 736-3310. (CD-ROM version available.)

Sauer, David. "Future NonShock." *Qualified Remodeler*, March 1993.

Index

P

packing and storing, 80–82
packing guidelines, 81
paint and wallcovering, 22, 25, 66, 90, 93, 95
payments, 63–64, 69, 98
permits, 16, 71–73
    fees, 73
    responsibility for obtaining, 71
    types of, 71–73
physically challenged, adaptations for, 7
plans, types of, 55–57
plumbing, 58, 59, 66, 90
plumbing fixtures, 22, 24–25
preconstruction meetings, 73–76
preliminary sketches, 52–53
product demonstrations, 96–97
product selection, 17
professional affiliations, of remodelers, 39
progress payments, 63–64, 113
punchlists, 93–94, 113

Q

qualifications of professional remodelers, 28, 36–37
Qualified Remodeler, trade magazine, 3

R

radio talk shows, for help finding a professional remodeler, 35
radon, 17, 113
rapport, with professional remodelers, 39–40
recreation areas, need to improve, 4
remodeling
    fever, 82, 83, 113
    ideas, 11–16, 57–60, 85–86
    process, 1
    tasks, 84, 87, 92–98
"Remodeling Blues" letter, 77
Remodeling magazine's "Cost Vs. Value" report, 49
Remodeling professionals, for remodeling ideas, 14

references, for professional remodelers, 38
refinancing, cash out, 44
reputation, of professional remodelers, 39
resale value, 48–49
retainage, 63–64, 98, 113
return-on-investment, 48–49
roofing and siding, 22, 24, 58, 59, 89

S

safety concerns, 31, 74, 75
scheduling, 29–30, 76, 78
scope of work, 62
security systems, need to improve, 6
selected bibliography, 115–16
seminars, for help finding a professional remodeler, 35
setback, 72, 113
siding, 22, 89
signage, 34; as delivery aid, 65
site preparation, 65, 84
software for remodeling ideas, 16
smoke detectors, 1, 96
specifications, 54, 65–66, 113
specialized activities, need to improve, 8
start and completion dates, 62–63
storage, need to improve, 5–6
storing and packing, 80–82
stoves, 23
subcontractors, 30, 64, 113
suppliers, for help finding a professional remodeler, 14

T

tax planning, 48
Tax Reform Act of 1986, 42
thermal and moisture protection, 66
traffic flow, 6
trim, 22, 23, 25
trade associations, of professional remodelers, 33, 36, 39
28–36 rule, 41

U

underground conditions, 18

V

vacation home, need for remodeling, 8
vacuum systems, central, 24
variance (zoning), 72–73, 113

W

warranties, 100–110
    duration, 103, 109–110
    express and implied, 101
    extent of coverage, 101
    insurance-backed, 109–110
    manufacturers', 109
    remodelers', 103–109
warranty cards, 97
weather, 17
windows, skylights, and doors, 22, 24,
    59, 65, 95
work schedule, 76, 78
workers' compensation insurance, 36,
    37, 62, 113
working conditions, 64–65
working drawings, 54, 113
workspace, setting aside, 20

Z

zoning, 72–73